Methodist Episcopal Church

Sixteenth Annual Report of the Freedmen's Aid Society

Of the Methodist Episcopal Church for 1883

Methodist Episcopal Church

Sixteenth Annual Report of the Freedmen's Aid Society
Of the Methodist Episcopal Church for 1883

ISBN/EAN: 9783337162429

Printed in Europe, USA, Canada, Australia, Japan

Cover: Foto ©ninafisch / pixelio.de

More available books at **www.hansebooks.com**

SIXTEENTH ANNUAL REPORT

OF THE

FREEDMEN'S AID SOCIETY

OF THE

METHODIST EPISCOPAL CHURCH,

FOR 1883.

CINCINNATI:
WESTERN METHODIST BOOK CONCERN PRESS.
1883.

CONTENTS.

PAGE.

REPORT OF THE CORRESPONDING SECRETARY, ... 3
   AGGREGATE COLLECTION greater than during any preceding year. It indicates growing interest in behalf of this cause, and the wisdom of the General Conference in enlarging the Society's sphere of action so as to embrace all the needy population of the South—Our schools are centers of elevating influence—Our graduates entering the learned professions, and engaging in useful pursuits—The great progress among this people, where schools are located, furnishes an argument for their general establishment.

CALL FOR ENLARGEMENT, ... 4
   WISDOM IN ORGANIZATION and administration—Wonderful success realized—The vastness and great needs of this field—The present aspects of the work—A large sum needed for both races—The possibilities opening before us.

THE YEAR'S WORK, ... 9
   SEVEN COLLEGES—Four Theological Schools—One Medical College—Fourteen Seminaries sustained—Total, twenty six.

NEW BUILDINGS, ... 10
   GAMMON THEOLOGICAL HALL—Philander Smith College—Little Rock University—Rust University—Morristown Seminary.

INDUSTRIAL DEPARTMENT, ... 15
   NEEDED THAT THIS PEOPLE may be fitted for the practical duties of life—These advantages can not be secured elsewhere—Their physical needs demand this training—These departments in successful operation at Clark and Claflin Universities.

SCHOOLS FOR WHITES, ... 22
   FIVE CHARTERED Institutions and fifteen Seminaries.

REPORT OF SCHOOLS IN THE SOUTH—BY BISHOP WILEY AND DR. RUST, 23
THREE EPOCHS, ... 33
CENTENNIAL OF AMERICAN METHODISM, ... 34
REPORT OF AUDITING COMMITTEE, ... 36
FINANCIAL STATEMENT, ... 37
CONFERENCE COLLECTIONS, ... 39
TREASURER'S REPORT, ... 41
SUMMARY OF ANNUAL DISBURSEMENTS, ... 51
SIXTEENTH ANNIVERSARY, ... 52
ADDRESS—*Our School Work*—BY PROF. W. H. CROGMAN, A. M., . . 52
ADDRESS—*Our Obligations to the Freedmen*—BY J. N. FITZGERALD, D. D. 63
ADDRESS—*The Black Woman of the South: Her Neglects and Her Needs*—BY REV. ALEXANDER CRUMMEL, D. D., ... 72
ADDRESS—*A Triple Alliance for the Rescue of the Race*—BY REV. W. V. KELLY, D. D., ... 86
ADDRESS—*The Methodist Episcopal Church in the South*—BY REV. J. M. WALDEN, LL. D., ... 97
ADDRESS—*The New South: What shall it be?*—BY REV. J. C. HARTZELL, D. D., ... 121

SIXTEENTH ANNUAL REPORT.

The Board of Managers of the Freedmen's Aid Society of the Methodist Episcopal Church respectfully submits its Sixteenth Annual Report.

The aggregate amount collected during the past year for our educational work in the South exceeds that of any preceding one in the Society's history. This is a fact of no little significance, when it is considered that each benevolent organization of the Church has made vigorous efforts to awaken a deeper interest in its chosen field of effort and increase contributions to its specific work.

For the Society to hold its own under such circumstances is all that could be expected, but to realize so marked an increase furnishes an occasion for joy and grateful acknowledgment. It indicates a growing interest in behalf of this benevolent enterprise of the Church, and a higher appreciation of the importance and magnitude of the work of educating emancipated millions who appeal to us in touching strains for teachers and ministers to aid them in their preparation to become good citizens and intelligent Christians. Yea, more—it indicates the people's confidence in the wisdom of the General Conference in recommending the enlargement of the Society's sphere of action, so as to embrace in its efforts the needy and ignorant youth of the South.

Our schools have been improved in the qualifications of the teachers, the attainments of the pupils, and in methods of government and instruction. Wherever a good school is established it becomes a center of power, enlightening the people and improving their morals, and those who avail themselves of its advantages secure the best preparation for a useful and happy life. Though many that attend school obtain but a very imperfect education, yet even a brief attendance imparts new views of life, and awakens in the mind bright hopes of usefulness and honor.

The number of students pursuing academic and collegiate studies in our schools is constantly increasing, and each year adds to the number and qualifications of our graduates. Already a few of our alumni are taking an active part in efforts for the world's redemption; thousands scattered over the South are engaged in teaching school; a few are reaping success as physicians; a smaller number are practicing law; some are editing newspapers, and others are securing for themselves recognition in the various departments of industrial and business pursuits. These first-fruits of our school work encourage us to expect rich and abundant harvests when our schools shall be supplied with a full corps of able instructors, commodious school buildings, suitable apparatus, and liberal endowments.

We can not refrain from adding our testimony to the wonderful improvement of this race in all the elements of Christian civilization, such as no other people in the history of the world ever secured in so brief a period of time. To the school, the pulpit, and the press this improvement is largely indebted. Occasionally some one utters a wail of despair at the deplorable condition of morals that prevails among this people in certain localities, but this wail calls forth stern rebuke from those familiar with the condition of the colored people in more favored portions of the country.

It is true that in some sections of the South many are still in gross darkness, but in other portions Churches have been planted, schools established, newspapers started, and the people, catching the quickening influence of intelligence and religion, have made remarkable progress in every department of Christian culture. We must not relax our efforts in this good work until there shall be accomplished throughout the entire South what has already been achieved where all our educational and religious agencies combined have secured their grandest triumphs.

CALL FOR ENLARGEMENT.

There are urgent demands for increased contributions to this cause, and we should be indifferent to the wants of the hour and untrue to great interests intrusted to us by the Master if we failed to voice distinctly and earnestly to the Church, for which this Society acts, the call which God is making for the permanent enlargement of our work in the South. Reasons enforcing this demand are various and urgent.

I. The wisdom evinced in the organization and administration of the affairs of this Society entitles it to confidence and consideration. No backward steps have been required to correct mistakes. Few, if any, serious ones have been made in selecting locations and sites for our institutions, plans for our buildings, professors to occupy them, and modes of administration. Without depreciating the judgment of those who have planned and managed this great interest, it is safe to say that its great success is due rather to divine guidance than human foresight. The field itself was new and difficult to cultivate. Facts necessary for intelligently working this field were wanting. The freedmen were restless, dissatisfied, persecuted, migratory. Those who showed them practical sympathy and help fell under the ban of proscription. Much, therefore, that was done, was done tentatively, and not by processes of intelligent, logical reasoning. The whole movement was providential. In nothing more than in the unity of administration, from the beginning, is the divine guidance seen, for the same Board of Management, with only a few changes, has been permitted to lay the foundations and build up this grand superstructure of beneficence for the freedmen.

II. Added to this is the wonderful success realized. The institutions planted have advanced from primary schools to seminaries and colleges, and from rudimental studies to those of a high grade. What was feeble has become strong. What was tentative has become established. Theory has become cheering fact. Experiment has become demonstration. The agencies employed, the work done, and the grand results achieved vindicate the claims of this Society to the confidence and support of the Church.

One hundred Christian teachers have been sustained in this work during the past sixteen years, eighty thousand pupils have been instructed in our schools, nine hundred and fifty thousand children have been taught by our teachers and our pupils who have become teachers, and four hundred and fifty thousand dollars have been expended in school property. The seal of God's approval has been placed upon this work, and this demands not only gratitude but greatly increased contributions.

Take into consideration the variety, the scope, and extent of this educational work in behalf of nearly seven millions of colored people in the South, seven chartered universities and colleges, four theological schools, one medical college, and fourteen seminaries, centrally located in the South, and you may get some faint conception of the vastness of the work inaugurated and the grand results thus early achieved by our Society.

III. Consider, also, the vastness of this field, and its great needs. In area the field of the Freedmen's Aid Society covers one-half that of the United States, the Territories excepted. Within this great area are more than one-third the entire population of the United States. Of the more than eighteen millions occupying the Southern States, six and a half million are freedmen. From forty to fifty-five per cent of the voters of these sixteen States are not able to read the ballots that they cast. Thirty per cent of the white population, and eighty per cent of the colored, can not read nor write.

The industrial and moral needs of these proscribed and debased people are even greater than their intellectual. They who yesterday were chattels, personal, and to-day are citizens, need the hand of care and kindness to guard and guide and help them to a better destiny than that to which slavery had consigned them. Christian citizenship and manhood are to be reinstated, where, so recently, they had been stamped out by the iron heel of slavery.

The vices and tendencies of two hundred years of barbarism need displacing by the virtues and refinement of a real Christian civilization. To effect this thoroughly and extensively will require persistent, costly work, and much of it. To attempt this, as the Methodist Episcopal Church did more than seventeen years ago, was no trifling undertaking. Less than sublime faith in God and in the power of Christianity would have been entirely inadequate to the undertaking and achievement of all that was demanded by these conditions.

We can scarcely fail to see that we have builded better than we knew, and we are astonished and delighted as we behold the growing greatness of this work. It is also discovered that to hold what has been gained, and to give it the largest and grandest crowning possible, will require far greater outlays than heretofore. This increase should begin at once and go rapidly forward.

IV. This call for enlargement is enforced by the present aspects of the work.

The last year's contributions show large advances upon those of former years, so demonstrating the continued and growing faith of the Church in the wisdom, economy, and safety of this agency. Nearly eight cents per member is now given by our membership. This is a large increase upon our gifts of four or five years ago, when they were only from four to five cents per member. One and a quarter millions of dollars have been expended by this Freedmen's Aid Society during the last decade and a half, say about eighty thousand dollars a year for sixteen years. This is no mean sum to lay on God's altar for His poor.

In permanent moral results may be reckoned the culture of thousands of colored men and women who are lifting up other less favored thousands into the clear light of Christian civilization. In material form these results are seen in the greater financial and physical thrift of the people lately down-trodden, and in college and school properties, which are there to stay and to have large fruitage in all time to come; and also in the thirty-six thousand dollars in endowment funds donated this year. This last is only the beginning of a large seeding, and of a still larger harvesting in similar lines. Since Jesus ascended from Bethany there was never a moment when the Church was making such grand progress as now, in all her enterprises, and in none of them is the success so great as in the work done for these freedmen. In none is the outlook more hopeful and promising.

But to meet this advance and to be in complete preparation for it upon an adequate scale, a liberal outlay is now demanded: in the character and improvement of educational facilities, in their increase and enlargement, in their more complete equipment with adequate teachers and professors, and in permanent endowments for this onward movement. Rev. E. H. Gammon has set a noble example by endowing a chair of theology in the Clark University, at Atlanta, Georgia, with the sum of twenty thousand dollars. If one hundred were to follow this good example the foundations laid would be none too large for the needs of the freedmen's work. Two million dollars ought to be forthwith consecrated to the improvement and endowment of the freedmen's institutions we already have. Let no one suppose this is a mere random statement. We have one hundred teachers and professors in our present institutions: but what are these among so many? For those already in the field there ought to be endowment funds of at least $1,600,000, so making higher education as nearly as possible free to the freedmen seeking it. For acquiring additional grounds, erecting new buildings, and improving those already existing, $400,000 will be found little enough. For the freedmen's institutions existing and demanded, and to man them for full and effective work, two million dollars is not an unreasonable estimate.

A large sum is also needed for the whites in the South, many of whom are lamentably illiterate; for the two universities inaugurated, one at Little Rock, Arkansas, with its new university building just completed at a cost of more than thirty thousand dollars, with more than a hundred students in its halls, and the other at Chattanooga, Tennessee, with its beautiful site purchased, and a donation from the citizens of fifteen thousand dollars to aid in the erection of a university building, to be completed at the earliest time possible, and for other institutions under the care of the Church, surely a like sum could be wielded most effectively.

All this should have early accomplishment. By His providence, by His wonderful blessing on what has already been done, by all forms of ability given to the Methodist people, God is saying, "'Go forward; enlarge the place of thy tent; and let them stretch forth the curtains of thine habitation; spare not; lengthen thy cords and strengthen thy stakes, for thou shalt break forth on the right hand and on the left.' Devise liberally. Plan and give and do, worthy of me, worthy of my claims upon you, worthy of the great gift of Jesus and all that it brings, worthy of the great possibilities opening before you."

By laying the whole work of higher education in the South among both colored and white people upon the Freedmen's Aid Society, the General Conference has shown confidence in the adaptability of this agency for this work, and has laid the responsibility of furnishing it with all needed means for doing it upon the heart and conscience of the Church, where it belongs.

V. The possibilities opening before us urgently demand this enlargement. Possible results to the present six and a half million of freedmen, and to the thirty millions they will soon become; possible results to the millions occupying the area and numbering the people of an empire,—a part of our nation, and through them to the one hundred millions, we are soon to be as a people; to the nation we love so well, and to the Church on which God has already put so much honor; to the dark continent of Africa, which for centuries has lifted imploring hands to God; and possible results in increasing revenues of glory to Jesus in this world and the next. In all this is a call for enlarged devotion and zeal and offerings for this cause, such as never summoned to any other similar charity.

The ratio of increase in educational and Church growth in the South for the last two decades, with the momentum acquired and with the enlarged facilities indicated, will give us by the close of the century nearly two millions of Church members in the South, as refined and educated as any equal number of Methodists in any part of the world; hundreds of well-trained missionaries in Africa, so giving an upward impulse to the two hundred millions of Africa which will evangelize them in a few decades and illume the "Dark Continent" with the light and love of heaven.

THE YEAR'S WORK.

We submit a brief report of what has been done the past year, the amount of money collected, and the purposes for which it has been expended.

Schools.

The Society has aided in the establishment and support of the following schools, seven of which are legally chartered with collegiate powers:

Chartered Institutions.

	No. Teachers.	No. Pupils.
Central Tennessee College, Nashville, Tenn.,	12	324
Clark University, Atlanta, Ga.,	6	225
Claflin University, Orangeburg, S. C.,	11	424
New Orleans University, New Orleans, La.,	6	231
Philander Smith College, Little Rock, Ark.,	5	136
Rust University, Holly Springs, Miss.,	6	367
Wiley University, Marshall, Texas.	6	313
	7	

Theological Schools.

Centenary Biblical Institute, Baltimore, Md.,	6	151
*Gammon Theological School, Atlanta, Ga.,	2	
*Baker Institute, Orangeburg, S. C.,		
*Gilbert Haven School of Theology, New Orleans, La.,		
	4	

Medical College.

Meharry Medical College, Nashville, Tenn.,	1	8	30

*Pupils enumerated in the other schools.

Institutions not Chartered.

	No. Teachers.	No. Pupils.
Bennett Seminary, Greensboro, N. C.,	6	153
Cookman Institute, Jacksonville, Fla.,	7	274
Forrest City School, Forrest City, Ark.,	2	62
Haven Normal School, Waynesboro, Ga.,	2	88
Huntsville Normal School, Huntsville, Ala.,	3	70
Houston Seminary, Houston, Texas,	3	109
La Grange Seminary, La Grange, Ga.,	2	100
Meridian Academy, Meridian, Miss.,	3	107
Morristown Seminary, Morristown, Tenn.,	3	130
New Hope Academy, New Hope, Texas,	1	52
Paris School, Paris, Texas,	2	52
Rome Normal School, Rome, Ga.,		
West Texas Conference Seminary, Austin, Tex.,		
West Tennessee Seminary, Mason, Tenn.,	3	139
	14	
Total Institutions 24,	105	3,537

In these institutions the number of pupils taught during the year is classified as follows:

Pupils.

Biblical,	304
Medical,	51
Collegiate,	145
Academic,	410
Normal,	1,387
Intermediate,	767
Primary,	473
Total,	3,537

NEW BUILDINGS.
Gammon Theological Hall.

The building for the accommodation of the students in theology, in connection with Clark University, has just been completed. It is a beautiful building, of Gothic architecture, one hundred and twelve feet long, and fifty-five feet wide. The basement story is built of light granite taken from our own quarry, and the other stories are constructed of brick burned at our brick-yard, scarcely a stone's throw distant from the structure, and the whole building is tastefully trimmed with cut stone. It is located in a grove of young trees, upon an eminence, commanding a fine view of Atlanta and the surrounding country.

Thanks to Bishop H. W. Warren and Rev. E. H. Gammon for this magnificent building for the training of our ministers for this vast section of our country. Bishop Warren has paid toward this building seventeen thousand five hundred dollars. Rev. E. H. Gammon donated seven thousand dollars, and the Freedmen's Aid Society paid two thousand dollars for the beautiful grounds upon which it is located, adjacent to the four hundred and fifty acres already owned by the Society. The furnishing of the building and the improvement of the grounds will require three thousand dollars, making the entire cost of this grand theological school and grounds thirty thousand dollars. This beautiful edifice, without a dollar's indebtedness, will, in a few weeks, be dedicated to Christian education and the specific training of young men to preach the unsearchable riches of Christ. To crown this enterprise Rev. E. H. Gammon has endowed the chair of theology in this institution by the payment of twenty thousand dollars to the treasurer of the Freedmen's Aid Society. Under the supervision of this Society this great educational enterprise of our Church was inaugurated at Atlanta, the gate-way city of the South, and under the same judicious management it has been conducted and developed to its present importance. It promises to become one of the most influential agencies of our Church in the South, not only for the training of ministers, teachers, and physicians, but also in providing for the young an opportunity to become good business men, mechanics, and farmers, that they may enter upon a successful career in life, properly prepared to secure respectability among their fellows and a competent support for their families.

Philander Smith College.

In 1876 a school was opened at Little Rock, Arkansas, by the Freedmen's Aid Society, and was taught first in a hired hall and then in an old meeting-house; and though it has been sustained for years under great embarrassments, it has accomplished great good in awakening an interest among the people for an education, and in furnishing teachers and preachers; and now the school has been transferred from a dilapidated church, in an unhealthy location, to a beautiful and convenient edifice, erected on a healthful and elevated site, commanding a full view of the city. The money to build this college was donated by Mrs. Adeline E. Smith, of Oak Park, Illinois, as a memorial of her deceased husband, who had taken the deepest interest in the emancipation of the slaves and the education of the freedmen. The school bore the name of Walden Seminary, in remembrance of Dr. Walden's valuable services in behalf of this Society—he having been one of its originators and its first corresponding secretary, while the present corresponding secretary was associated with him in the organization of the Society and served the Church in the office of field superintendent. Dr. Walden learning of the interest of Mrs. Smith in the education of this emancipated people, and her liberal purposes in regard to it, and that she was favorably inclined toward Little Rock, visited her, and urged her to adopt the Seminary, and establish in its place a college to bear the name of her deceased husband.

This is one of the most attractive buildings erected by the Society. It combines conveniences of the school and the home, and affords accommodations for more than a hundred students. The influence of this college edifice will be felt all through the South-west, awakening interest in improved school architecture, and in educating youth for the noble purposes of life. The site, building, and furnishing cost over fifteen thousand dollars, and the property is free from debt.

Little Rock University.

Our Society has just completed, at Little Rock, Arkansas, the best building it has erected, and it is pronounced the handsomest and most complete school edifice in the South-west. The building is four stories. The basement is constructed of stone, the other stories of brick, and every part of it is finished in a thorough and workmanlike manner. This city, selected as the most desirable in all respects for the location of the university, is central to a large range of territory, where there are no institutions of learning of a high grade, and this one is designed to meet the educational demands of the Methodist Episcopal Church throughout this section of the country, and furnish the advantages for any desiring to obtain a first-class academic, collegiate, or professional education. The university is located on Lincoln Avenue, on a bluff of the Arkansas River, opposite the Union Depot, only a short distance from it, and is in full view of all persons passing through Little Rock on the cars. This building has been erected at a cost of thirty-five thousand dollars; and the former residence of Governor Powell, now used for a boarding-house, and the thirteen acres of ground adjoining, cost fifteen thousand dollars, making a total cost for this property of fifty thousand dollars.

The university has opened in the new building, under the presidency of Rev. George W. Gray, D. D., an able and experienced educator, assisted by a corps of professors distinguished for their attainments as scholars and for their thoroughness and success as educators. It is hoped that the debt upon the institution may be speedily liquidated, so that it may be dedicated to Christian culture free from all embarrassment.

It must be remembered that only the money contributed for the specific purpose of erecting buildings can be devoted to that object, as the collections of the conferences are expended in salaries for the teachers and in current expenses for the schools.

Rust University.

The university was chartered by the Legislature of Mississippi, in June, 1870, and has since been in successful operation. For the past few years it has suffered greatly for the want of accommodations, having only one small two-story school building for nearly three hundred students. Through the liberality of J. J. H. Gregory, of Marblehead, Massachusetts, George I. Seney, of Brooklyn, New York, and others, a large and commodious college building was commenced, more than a year ago, and has just been completed by our Society, free from debt. It is a fine four-story brick structure, one hundred and ten feet long, and forty feet deep, with slate roof finish, modern school improvement, and the most approved appointments. It admirably combines boarding and school conveniences, has excellent rooms for the faculty, a large chapel, dining-room, kitchen, laundry, etc. It cost twenty-three thousand dollars, and is a model for cheapness, construction, and beauty.

The State of Mississippi must have, for a long time to come, an immense colored population, for in 1880 there were 650,291 colored and 479,398 white citizens. Methodism is permeating with its influence this large population; and, if it had the means, it would control the moral and spiritual destiny of this people. The great peril that threatens our work here comes from the designing influences of Romanism. At this place, and all over the State, the Romanists are making every effort to convert the colored race to their own faith. They seize upon the opportunities of the hour, and, with effort and sacrifice worthy of a better cause, seek to bring this people under the power of the Vatican. Christian education can meet this enemy of freedom and progress, and protect this unfortunate race from the perils of Romanism.

Our lamented Bishop Gilbert Haven, speaking of the location of this institution, said: "Our school at Holly Springs stands on a lot of twenty acres, where General Grant's batteries were placed when he captured the town. Some might fancy Grant's battery was there now. It is a pretty site—the best in town. It overlooks the place, and is the worthy cap-stone of its present and future. About one hundred acres also belong to the institution, separated from the campus by only an intervening lot of about fifteen acres. On the sightliest point of this sightly knoll stands the imposing brick building now known as the Rust University. It has begun right. It has the right location, lands, and ideas, and faith. The Freedmen's Aid Society has done much, for which the Church will hold it in grateful remembrance. This work is among its best. Those who pass southward over the 'great Jackson route' should stop over a train at Holly Springs. If they can not do that they can see the university building as they pass, and can give to its necessities. Help the cause in this redeemed State! Educate these people for their liberties and duties! They will repay your gifts a million-fold in the uplifting of their pleasant liberty, in true knowledge and righteousness, and in their contributions to the elevation of the whole nation."

Morristown Seminary.

The new building at Morristown, Tennessee, is a substantial and commodious edifice, conveniently located on a pleasant eminence, and its architecture and finish are highly creditable to the judgment and taste of the architect and builder. It is fifty-seven by fifty-eight feet, has twenty-two rooms, and will accommodate fifty boarders. There are separate apartments for the sexes, and every thing is adjusted to the wants of the school. The building cost twenty-six hundred dollars, and the furniture cost four hundred dollars, making three thousand dollars. This school is central to a large population needing educational advantages, and the new building supplies a long felt want for suitable accommodations in this part of the South. The seminary is within the bounds of the East Tennessee Conference, and its ministers take the deepest interest in its prosperity. Great credit is due to the Rev. J. S. Hill, the principal, for his earnest efforts in the establishment and support of this school and the erection of this new building. A few hundred dollars are needed to pay the balance due the builder, and I know of no place where such an amount of money can be invested in the cause of education where it will accomplish so great good in so brief a time.

INDUSTRIAL DEPARTMENT.

In several of our institutions an industrial department has been introduced, and the students have been trained in the workshop and on the farm, as our means would allow. Out of study hours, in term-time and in vacation, under the guidance of practical teachers, the young men are acquiring skill in the use of tools, and the young women in household duties and economy. The work is but begun, and small and feeble is its present day. But the conception contains an idea of unlimited expansibility, already proven to be of the highest utility, and if encouraged by the patrons of the Society, and the friends of the freedmen, is destined to achieve the largest success. Already, on the magnificent property at Atlanta, the young men are learning to practice skill in agriculture; neat buildings erected by their hands attest their readiness in the use of carpenter's tools; and the hammer and saw, the forge and the printer's case, are opening to them new avenues of education, independence, and wealth.

The following reasons may be offered as a justification of our entrance upon this work of industrial education:

First. We should aid the industrial training of the freedmen so as to make their education as broad as education ought to be. That means more than book learning to a man who has a living to earn and a place of usefulness to fill in society. No doubt, the first great necessity of the freedmen was represented in their first great desire—to learn to read. The opening of the mind to ideas is next in fact and importance to the opening of the heart to God. So they rushed to our schools to learn books. Then, with their small acquirements, they hurried forth to teach the precious elements of knowledge to others, and at the same time to earn a little money on which to live and by which to secure further education. The amount of money appropriated to schools in the Southern States, in proportion to the population, is still very small. The wages these teachers can earn are meager. And as the number increases of such as have ability to teach their fellows, the need grows more apparent that some other ability than that of teaching should be developed in the students at our schools. The method of their education must not leave them incapable of exerting their energies and employing their talents upon any and all forms of industry, by which they can at once benefit their people and educate themselves.

In addition, and in harmony with the foregoing, we can but agree that education should be a road to independence. While, generally speaking, the demand for trained brains, North and South, takes up the supply, there is always sure to be a demand for trained hands in all departments of manufacture and labor. All men can not be teachers; not every man should try to be. But all men can and ought to do something useful to society. The man of the common people has, no doubt, a degree of superiority and independence when versed only in books, but much more has he when, with that intelligence directing his hands, he can cut out a coat, shoe a horse, build a wagon, or erect a house. The education of the freedmen to manhood should, therefore, comprehend industrial training, before it can be called a complete or even a suitable education.

Second. They should be taught handicraft at our schools, because they can not be well and fairly taught anywhere else. Remember that the manufacturing industries of the South scarcely had an existence until after the war. The people were an agricultural people. Their agriculture was rude and (on account of slave labor) unprofitable. For this there were many causes. Only a small part of the population worked, and these were mostly slaves. Being slaves, their labor was made a badge of degradation, and so the number of voluntary laborers was diminished. Nearly all kinds of work were rudely done, because the slave was not permitted to get that instruction which could make him a skilled laborer. If he could have made a lock, he could have used the key to take off his fetters. Unlike the farmer of the North, whose leisure was spent in such reading and arts as would improve his skill and his farming, the slave had no opportunity to learn what dexterity was shackled in his hand.

All the world knows that the skilled mechanism of America is not invented in the South. The inventions which have made the wealth of that section were not produced by artisans of her own. So, nearly all the slaves were rude farmers, and knew little besides. And now, in these days of freedom, what are the actual and possible occupations of the colored man in the South? Except teaching and preaching, his are only the most menial employments. He is a laborer, a porter, a waiter, a barber, a driver, a rude smith, or a clumsy joiner. He is rarely a cabinet maker, a machinist, a watch maker, or any thing that involves the training of his hand to skill and his head to inventiveness. Nor can he command the facilities by which to improve his skill. Few in the South are able to teach him; fewer are willing to do it, under conditions favorable to his apprenticeship and his manhood. If the colored people are to learn trades and arts, under any thing like advantages equal to those enjoyed by Northern apprentices, they must learn them at Northern hands. And where? Not in the North, whither they can not go, *but in our schools*.

Third. Their physical needs also demand this industrial education; and, indirectly, but equally, their intellectual and spiritual needs. With freedom came the need of decent houses, furniture, implements of all sorts—agricultural and mechanical, wagons, harnesses, every thing. They need books and papers, houses of worship, school-houses; in fact, the catalogue of their actual wants is almost endless. Any thing that free civilization uses, they are in want of. And how shall they be supplied? Until they themselves acquire the skill to make what they need, those needs will never be supplied. Think how primitive and insufficient are all their resources; so much so that in their poverty they can not accumulate money with which to buy all these fittings of freedom. But their possible sources of wealth are in the heart, the head, the hand. They have ability to labor and to acquire skill, and that capacity should be made use of to elevate them to comfort and refinement. Part of their idleness, or that of any rude people, may be justly credited to their lack of diverse, interesting, and remunerative employments. Their houses are often hovels; their clothing, the coarsest and poorest; their churches, rude and uncomfortable; their farming implements, such as to multiply the difficulties and diminish the profits of agriculture. So that they may acquire these necessaries they should be taught how to erect houses, make furniture, wield the hammer, build machinery, invent implements, weave cloth, set type, and every other manual trade. While they are acquiring these arts, they are becoming educated and elevated, they are earning wages, growing more useful to society, commanding the social and political rank of skilled and invaluable labor, and improving in every condition necessary to a useful and happy existence as members of human society.

Fifty thousand dollars could be judiciously invested at each of our universities by which to evoke facilities that would make instruction in these trades possible, if not compulsory, to every student. And just as necessary as mechanical trades, in that marvelous garden spot—that South, with its unbounded agricultural possibilities—the farmers should be taught to make their land yield the largest crops of the best products. Thus, with the very fruits of their apprenticeship, on the wide lands of our schools, the students would maintain health, ward off idleness, cultivate industry, and raise the food which would supply their boarding house table, thus earning an education. This would be worth to them more by far than an education given as a gratuity.

In such an industrial home, also, as our Society has begun in Atlanta and Orangeburg, if provided with increased facilities, the young women would learn to do a hundred things to increase the comfort of their own homes; to cook, to sew, to make tasteful garments, to adorn their rooms, so causing, in a coming generation, a complete revolution in the home life of the freed people. All this might be done in an extensive model home for girls.

To further this well begun work, what is needed at these schools? They want a competent superintendent of the farm, who has also mechanical skill, to be at once an instructor in agriculture and mechanics. They want tools of approved pattern—carpenters', machinists', printers'. And the most economical way to furnish these aids to the work is to give the money to the institutions or the Society, and let them procure what they want. They know precisely what would be the most serviceable. Their necessities and experience have shown them. Liberally assisted now, at the beginning, the income of the department would soon pay its expenses. Let some one, or several, give a donation of ten thousand dollars for the founding of the industrial department at each of our universities. Let this money be applied to its use, under the advice of the officers of the Freedmen's Aid Society, the president of the school, and the donor himself. On that corner-stone could be built up a great industrial system of education for the people, and a great people for the nation.

Clark University.

About three years ago, chiefly by the efforts of Bishop Warren, a beginning was made of an industrial department. A few sets of tools were purchased, and several very cheap buildings erected by the students, as a first lesson. For the want of means the work progressed slowly; however, an engine and several machines were added, and steady advance was made, till, at the end of two years, the department attracts general attention. Visitors are shown, in the shop, original plans and specifications, well made joints, and skillfully turned objects of use and ornaments; and out of doors more advanced lessons in the form of three fine cottages.

Our aim is not only to teach trades by which the students may obtain a living, for we believe the human intellect capable and worthy of something higher than a merely "practical education." But, knowing the circumstances of the majority of our pupils, we desire that the training of the mind shall not unfit them for the "stern realities" of life. More than this, the head can be reached successfully by the nerves of skilled hands as well as by the optic or aural fibers.

By the aid of a generous portion of the Slater Fund, it is our purpose to build steadily and thoroughly on the foundations so well laid. The best plans for conducting this important department have not yet been discovered, but must be born of experience. The plan as now developed, and the work accomplished, can best be summarized under each department.

1. WOOD WORK.

The shop contains an engine, which furnishes power for two saws, three lathes, a scroll saw, and a printing press. The pupils first learn the use of hammer, saw, and plane; then they are advanced to mechanical drawing and the production of finer work on the lathe and scroll saw. We manufacture our own tables, erect our frame buildings, saw out scroll work for ornamental work of the cottages, and turn croquet sets and base-ball bats, for the recreation hours. In this way the lessons are made of practical value.

2. THE FARM.

A practical farmer has begun this year to make this department what it should be. Students are learning to grade and beautify the campus, to raise flowers and trees, and to employ the best methods in cultivation of the soil. Young men who are unable to pay for a full course of study are thus enabled to obtain healthful employment, the rudiments of an English education, a better knowledge of modern agriculture, and at the same time furnish the boarding-house with a better variety of food.

3. Domestic Economy.

The "model home" idea, which had its origin here, and has since been adopted by other colleges, is in successful operation. A neat cottage of six rooms, erected by our carpenters, neatly furnished by friends in the North, makes a pleasant home for six young ladies, who, under the direction of a matron, "keep house" after the most approved methods. Besides the "home," all the girls of the school are organized into classes, for sewing, dress-cutting and making, and millinery.

4. Printing Office.

The printing office is supplied with a press and all necessary material. A class of young men and women, under charge of a teacher, edit, set up, and print a weekly paper, called the *Elevator*. We find it one of the best means of promoting quickness and accuracy. By the close of the present year we expect to be able to do all the printing needed at the university.

5. Iron Work.

In a small building we have forges and full sets of tools, and have done a great deal of our own iron work. It is our intention at once to secure a competent teacher and necessary machinery.

6. Business Department.

A teacher of long and successful experience will open a thorough business course at the beginning of the Winter term. The usual studies of such a course will be prosecuted, especial attention being given in this, as in other departments, to the probable circumstances in which our students will be placed in the coming years.

In all the various developments of this industrial plan, from its inception till now, Bishop Warren has been an enthusiastic helper and invaluable adviser, and Rev. E. O. Thayer, president of the university, has taken the deepest interest and has co-operated most efficiently. We earnestly invite friends visiting Atlanta to call at the university and see for themselves; and all others interested will receive prompt replies to all inquiries by mail. Dr. Haygood, while inspecting our shops, exclaimed: "The half has not been told me."

Claflin University.

The Agricultural College and Mechanical Institute of South Carolina have been connected, for several years, with the Claflin University, located at Orangeburg, South Carolina; and the conduct and administration of their affairs placed under the charge of the Rev. Edward Cooke, D. D., the president of our university. Dr. Cooke is a Christian gentleman, an excellent scholar, and an experienced educator, and under his wise management great harmony has prevailed between the university and the industrial departments of the State; and a large number of students have been aided in defraying their expenses by work on the farm and in the shop. Valuable information has been imparted to the young men in agricultural pursuits and mechanic arts, and habits of industry and economy have been formed, which will be of great value to them in the industrial pursuits of life.

1. A Farm

Of one hundred and fifty acres of land. About one-half is under cultivation, and stocked with the necessary appliances for working it with success. Students labor under the direction of a superintendent, and thus defray, in part, the expense of their education.

2. Industrial Mechanics.

A carpenter's shop has been a feature of this college for years past. A new and larger shop is about to be erected, supplied with necessary machinery, for introducing some other manufacturing industry, in addition to carpentry. Students receiving the benefit of the funds devoted to this form of industry are expected to labor a portion of each working day, and to acquire a competent knowledge of the mechanical branches taught. To secure this object a skilled superintendent is employed.

3. Industrial Home for Girls.

An experienced matron is in charge of this department, who will give personal attention to the welfare of those under her care. Girls are taught the art of cooking, and the industries necessary for making their own homes comfortable and happy.

SCHOOLS FOR WHITES.

The last General Conference instructed the Managers of the Freedmen's Aid Society to render such assistance to schools for the whites as it could without embarrassment to its work among the colored people. In accordance with this instruction the Society has aided in establishing schools, and in sustaining those already in operation, to the extent of the instruction given and the ability possessed. The result shows that this action instead of diminishing appropriations for the colored work has largely increased them, furnishing the Society, by its additional claims for the enlargement of its work among the ignorant and needy of both races, funds to sustain in a healthful condition schools for the colored people and to inaugurate as speedily as possible a good system of education for the whites.

The plan of the Society is to establish a system of education, including two colleges, one for the South-west and the other for the Central South; academies located in various sections, easy of access for our membership, feeders for our colleges and agencies for the education and elevation of the people. In harmony with this plan, a university has been established at Little Rock, Arkansas, which is now in successful operation, and the other, at Chattanooga, Tenn., is progressing rapidly, and it is to be hoped that the new university building will be completed and ready for occupancy at the commencement of the next school year. Such aid and encouragement are given to our associated institutions as our funds will allow, and we most earnestly appeal for aid in sustaining this important department of educational work. A most encouraging beginning has been made in the establishment of a system of schools of various grades for this section of the country, which promises the most gratifying results to our Church and the nation.

Chartered Institutions.

	No. Teachers.	No. Pupils.
Andrews Collegiate Institute, Andrews Institute, Ala.,	3	113
Chattanooga University, Chattanooga, Tenn., (not yet chartered),		
East Tennessee Wesleyan University, Athens, Tenn.,	8	214
Little Rock University, Little Rock, Ark.,	10	206
Texas Wesleyan College, Fort Worth, Texas,	6	100

Institutions not Chartered.

	No. Teachers.	No. Pupils.
Baldwin Seminary, Baldwin, La.,	2	50
Brown Seminary, Leicester, N. C.,	1	62
Chandler College, Asheville, N. C.,		
Dickson Seminary, Dickson, Tenn.,		
Ellijay Seminary, Ellijay, Ga.,	2	100
Holston Seminary, New Market, Tenn.,	6	137
Harrison Seminary, Harrison, Ark.,	1	31
Kingsley Seminary, Bloomingdale, Tenn.,	4	136
Mount Union Seminary, Mount Union, Ala.,	1	61
Powell's Valley Seminary, Well Spring, Tenn.,	3	170
Rheatown Academy, Rheatown, Tenn.,		
Sequachee College, Tenn.,		
Texarkana Gymnasium, Texarkana, Ark.,	5	190
Tullahoma College, Tullahoma, Tenn.,		
West Tennessee Seminary, Hollow Rock, Tenn.,	5	98
	15 —	—
Total Institutions 19,	57	1,668

The above system of schools includes five colleges—one in Alabama, two in the South-east, another in the South-west, and the fifth in Texas; and fifteen seminaries tributary to these colleges.

OUR SCHOOLS IN THE SOUTH.

THE Executive Committee of the Freedmen's Aid Society at its meeting, January 3d, requested Rev. Bishop Wiley, the President of the Society, and Dr. Rust, the Corresponding Secretary, to visit its schools in the South, make a careful examination of them, and furnish a detailed report in writing to the Committee of their investigations. They spent four weeks in their tour of visitation, and at a meeting of the Committee, held March 2d, they submitted their report, of which the following is the substance:

REPORT ON OUR SCHOOLS IN THE SOUTH.

CENTRAL TENNESSEE COLLEGE.

At Nashville we have six buildings: A dwelling-house, occupied by the president, and largely used for the purposes of the school; a commodious chapel, capable of seating three hundred and fifty, over which are dormitories for students; a boarding-hall and dormitories; a dining-hall, with capacity for one hundred students; a large four-story building for recitation rooms on two floors, and dormitories in the two upper stories. These are all substantially built brick buildings, and are kept in a good state of repair. On a lot opposite these buildings has been recently erected a one-story frame building for the model school.

The college has enrolled one hundred and ninety-seven students, and about fifty in the model school. But on account of an alarm arising from a case of varioloid of one of the students, about fifty were absent from school, and it is supposed that nearly that many more were deterred from entering the school by the same cause. We attended recitations in classes ranging from the primary grade in the model school to the higher mathematics and advanced Greek and Latin, and were gratified with the character of the teaching and the evident industry and attainments of the students. The students were about equally divided between males and females, many of them well advanced in age and development. A number of the young men were looking to the ministry; a larger number were preparing for teachers, and a considerable number of the females were contemplating teaching.

MEHARRY MEDICAL COLLEGE.

Crowning an adjoining hill, a short distance south, we have a fine brick building, three stories high, with large lecture-room, ample accommodations for the dean's family, and all necessary appurtenances of a complete medical school. A frame building on the same premises furnishes good accommodations for anatomical purposes. This is pronounced by competent judges to be one of the most complete buildings for medical purposes in the South.

This is the only thoroughly organized medical school in the Mississippi Valley, south of the Ohio River, where colored persons can pursue this study, and when it is remembered that in this same territory there are about four millions of colored people, there is great reason that this school should be rendered most efficient by liberal endowment and thorough equipment for its important work.

Twenty-six promising young men we found attending regular instructions in the medical school. We were much pleased with the evidences of thoroughness in the course and the instructions given in the medical department. A full three years' course is required, and recitations regularly in all the departments are exacted. The medical education will compare well with the best medical schools of the land, and in view of the constant recitations and examinations the graduates will take a high place among medical students in the exactness and thoroughness of their knowledge. It has graduated twenty-three, who are engaged in the practice of medicine, and are meeting with encouraging success. The title of the property is vested in the Freedmen's Aid Society. They have, in all the departments, a force of ten teachers.

RUST UNIVERSITY.

On Saturday, January 27th, we reached Holly Springs, Mississippi, and remained till Tuesday morning. The Sabbath was spent in services among the students and people in the church. Here we found a large and beautiful tract of land, containing about fifteen acres, in a commanding position, overlooking the town. On this ground we have a pleasant frame building, occupied by the president and his family, and the old college building, being a two-story brick, seventy by forty feet, the lower floor divided into recitation rooms, the entire floor above used for chapel and recitations.

While we were visiting this institution there was a unanimous vote requesting that this building should hereafter be called McDonald Hall, in honor of the Rev. A. C. McDonald, who devoted years of earnest thought and labor to the interests of this school, and who died in the forefront of the battle.

We examined thoroughly a new building just completed by the Adams Brothers, of Chattanooga. This is a large and commanding brick edifice, one hundred feet long and forty deep, with a projecting T for chapel and other purposes, and is four stories high, with slate roof finish. It has ample accommodations for both boarding and school purposes for one hundred and fifty resident students, with excellent rooms for the faculty, a large chapel, dining-room, kitchen, laundry, etc. The whole building is admirably arranged for its purposes, and is an edifice creditable in every way to our Society. It cost about twenty thousand dollars, and is a model of cheapness for the style and character of the building. It is supposed to be one of the best school buildings in the State. The whole property of this institution is held by the Freedmen's Aid Society.

There were enrolled one hundred and sixty students, of whom forty were out engaged in teaching during the Winter months, and who will return to the school in March. About four hundred have gone out from this school, and are now engaged in teaching. Many of the best men in the Mississippi Conference have received more or less education in this institution. A large proportion of the present students are looking to a life in the ministry, or in teaching. We listened to recitations of classes in all grades, from primary studies to advanced mathematics and classics, and were specially pleased with the work, and gratified with the general instruction. A class of four is preparing for graduation. The management of the institution is careful, prudent, and thorough. There are six teachers employed in all the departments.

PHILANDER SMITH COLLEGE.

On Wednesday, January 31st, we reached Little Rock, Arkansas, and spent two days there. Here we found two institutions. The college is for colored students, and at present is held in the audience-room of the church. About ninety students are on the roll, and of this number about seventy are in attendance. The place for holding the school was very inconvenient, and yet we found good work in instruction by two instructors. The branches taught were those of a good English education. We so far felt the necessity for better accommodations for this school that we were on the verge of ordering the

Adams Brothers to go on at once with both buildings. Just then we saw a providential opening in the donation made by the heirs of Philander Smith, of ten thousand dollars for the erection of a building, and we immediately ordered the contractors to go forward with the new edifice. This lifts us over a delicate and serious embarrassment. For the future purposes of the school we have a tract in the city, embracing half a square, and in a most desirable situation, on elevated ground, in the midst of the population whom we wish to reach, and near to the new church which they are about completing. A building, very neat and very excellently designed, to cost ten thousand five hundred dollars, is to be at once erected, and will be ready for occupancy at the opening of the next school year. Our people are thoroughly satisfied with this arrangement, and are delighted with their prospects for the future. All parties are now working in harmony.

LITTLE ROCK UNIVERSITY.

On a very eligible site in this enterprising place, commanding a fine view of the city and its surroundings, we have a tract of land, containing about fourteen acres, on which is an elegant building, formerly the residence of Governor Clayton, and which is well adapted as a residence for the president and a part of the faculty of our university. A building of large proportions is being erected, the foundation of which we found completed, and the bricks burned, and the work rapidly progressing. This will be a commodious building, wholly devoted to college purposes and a residence for one of the professors. It will cost thirty thousand dollars. This is an enterprise which we have undertaken under the directions given to us by the late General Conference, to enter, as far as we might be able, into educational work among the whites. The building is to be completed in time for the opening of the next school year. The citizens are taking great interest in this institution, and have already contributed toward this building eight thousand dollars, and promise to make it fifteen thousand dollars.

The first session of the school has opened in the "Methodist Block," in the city, making use of three rooms in this building, and nearly one hundred students are enrolled, representing various academic and collegiate classes. Several young men, in their eagerness to get education, and in the absence of better accommodation, have come in from abroad, and are rooming in the unfinished attic of the building. These facts indicate the speedy success of the institution when we shall be able to use the new edifice. Under the inspiration of this new movement a preparatory school has been established at Texarkana, where two hundred students are in attendance, some of them preparing for the university, and others for teaching and the duties of life. There is good prospect that as soon as we get into working order we will be able to inaugurate the various university departments of theology, law, medicine, and music. This movement is a very happy and important one, and is destined to meet a great and obvious need in the work of education in all this region, there being no similar institution in this whole section of country. It has given new inspiration to our Church work in the whole State.

WILEY UNIVERSITY.

We reached Marshall, Texas, the 1st of February, where another of our colleges is located. We have here a fine site overlooking the village, and about twenty acres of ground, on which there is a frame house, occupied by the president; a small cottage, occupied by one of the professors; and a two-story building, for boarding and dormitory purposes; and two brick buildings, two stories high, each about fifty by forty feet. They are substantial buildings, but somewhat out of repair, and defective in the construction of their roofs, for which some remedy must be found at an early day. After carefully investigating the condition of the buildings, and ascertaining the absolute necessity of additional accommodations for the students, we suggest that a mansard roof be placed upon each of these buildings, which will protect our property and obviate the necessity of any additional expensive buildings for years to come. There are one hundred and twenty-five students in the institution, gathered from various portions of the Southwest. We spent the day in examining the classes, which ranged all the way from preparatory to collegiate. There is also a primary school of nearly one hundred children, taught by one of the students of an advanced class, who thus defrays his expenses in securing his own education. There are four teachers here, and additional force should be added as soon as the finances of the Society will allow. This property belongs to the Freedmen's Aid Society.

HOUSTON SEMINARY.

We spent the 4th and 5th days of February in Houston, Texas. Here we have a new enterprise, opened the present year, for the accommodation of which we have purchased a valuable property in a central part of the city, costing seventy-five hundred dollars, and have opened the school with eighty pupils. This school is more than three hundred miles distant from our university at Marshall, and is in the midst of a dense population of colored people, and meets a necessity of another great region of this vast State. The grounds are high, and are sufficient for the erection of such additional buildings as may become essential to make this a first-class seminary. The deed for this property is held by the Freedmen's Aid Society.

BALDWIN SEMINARY.

On our way to New Orleans we spent a day at La Teche, Louisiana, visiting our seminary for the whites there.

We have here a beautiful property of twenty acres, donated by the venerable John Baldwin, on which is a convenient building occupied by the principal, and a pleasant cottage occupied by Brother Baldwin during his pleasure. We have also on this ground a two-story brick building for school purposes, the lower story being divided into four recitation rooms, and the upper being used for school and Church purposes. There is also a substantial new frame building erected for a boarding department. This property is pleasantly situated on the bayou, and the campus is mostly covered by a beautiful grove. The school, at present, is small, but the surroundings are promising, and there will probably develop here an important center for the education of white students. It is expected that this enterprise will become largely self-sustaining.

NEW ORLEANS UNIVERSITY.

On the 7th of February we arrived in this city. Our school property is centrally located, on the corner of Camp and Race Streets, fronting a pleasant park. It consists of two frame buildings, two stories high, and of sufficient capacity to meet the immediate necessities of the school, but the time will soon come when these somewhat dilapidated houses must give place to a building adequate to the growing wants of this institution. We ordered certain repairs to be made, the buildings to be painted, and encouraged the teachers to toil on in patience and hope. The school is in every respect in good condition, and excellent work is being done by teachers and students. The college has already graduated several classes of good scholars and useful workers. One hundred and seventy pupils are in attendance, in classes of various grades and attainments, and this number might soon be doubled if we could offer suitable accommodations. Five teachers are employed here.

CLARK UNIVERSITY.

On Saturday, February 10th, we arrived at Atlanta, and left on the evening of the 12th. Here we have one of our largest and most flourishing enterprises. We have four hundred and fifty acres of ground, about twenty acres of which are inclosed for college purposes. A large portion of the land is wooded, and the whole of it well adapted for farming purposes, and this use should be made of it. We would, therefore, recommend to the Board to consider favorably the question of putting on this ground an intelligent and experienced farmer, to take charge of the grounds, and give employment to such students as may desire and need it, in cultivating the farm. This would greatly improve and add to the value of the ground, would furnish at a moderate rate supplies to the institution, and would be a great help to a number of students, who must either thus find some remunerative employment or go elsewhere to find it. It would also be in keeping with the line of policy pursued by the college in other departments.

We have here a large, commodious, substantial brick building, of three stories and basement, which cost thirty thousand dollars. It is our best building, is admirably adapted to all the wants of the school and boarding department, and is one of the best school edifices in the South. There is also a very pleasant and commodious house for the residence of the president. A neat cottage furnishes a home for one of the professors. A blacksmith shop and carpenter shop give employment and opportunity to the students to learn useful trades. A model home is being built for the purpose of giving the girls lessons in home-making and housekeeping. All these buildings, except the college, are of wood, and have been mainly built by the students, thus giving them employment and furnishing us the buildings at a comparatively moderate expense.

There are in the university one hundred students, nearly all of whom are from abroad, and are boarders in the institution, the property being too far distant from the city for the accommodation of local day students. The school is well governed; the instruction is careful and thorough; the students are industrious and in earnest; the order is excellent; the boarding department is neat and clean. The Church and our Society have good reason to be thankful that we are in possession of so excellent an educational institution, and one which promises so much for the future. There are seven teachers in the college proper, and one professor in charge of the industrial department, and a matron for the boarding department.

GAMMON THEOLOGICAL INSTITUTION.

Under the sanction of our Committee a beautiful knoll of nine acres, adjoining our own grounds, had been purchased for the Theological Institute. We found a space cleared away for the building, and were shown, by the contractor, the plans for the structure. It will be an imposing building, to cost about twenty-two thousand dollars, for which the funds have been nearly raised by Bishop Warren, one-third of which is donated by Mr. Gammon. The contract is made and the work is begun, and it is to be completed by the commencement of the next year. Mr. Gammon also secures to it an endowment of twenty thousand dollars, which is to be available as soon as the school opens. When this edifice shall be completed we shall have on our property at Atlanta a combination of buildings and educational facilities unsurpassed by any thing in the whole South, except the Vanderbilt University.

CLAFLIN UNIVERSITY.

On Tuesday, February 13th, we reached Orangeburg, South Carolina, the seat of our university for this State. We have here an excellent property, with ample grounds and eligibly located. The main building is a large, four-story brick edifice, used for chapel, school-rooms, and dormitories. A frame cottage, used for boarding-house, and several buildings for grammar school, scientific department, and primary school, are located on the grounds. The South Carolina Agricultural College is located here, in connection with our university. It has a large farm, which furnishes students an opportunity to aid in their expenses, and the State appropriates six thousand dollars each year toward the support of the school, under the direction of the president of the university. This aids in giving stability and efficiency to the institution. A carpenter shop also gives opportunity to students to learn a useful trade. Exclusive of the primary school, which is run as the public school of the city, there are one hundred and seventy students in the college. The whole presents the appearance of a busy hive of workers, and every thing looks like health and efficiency. The management is admirable and thorough. Instruction is given in all grades. A promising class is ready for graduation at the close of the year. We heard this class in mathematics, philosophy, and classics, and we would not be ashamed of them in any institution. The university here will take first rank among the best of our colleges. There are eight instructors in the school. The property is held by the Freedmen's Aid Society.

Finding that a trip to Florida would consume a whole week, and involve large expense, in visiting a single institution, we abandoned a visit to Cookman Institute.

BENNETT SEMINARY.

One of our best schools we found at Greensboro, North Carolina. We have a good three-story brick building, well adapted for academy or seminary purposes. It is well conducted, and instruction is given in preparatory and academic studies. The president and teachers are enthusiastic, and the students are earnest. It is a good institution, doing first-rate work. There are one hundred students. The grounds contain about twenty-five acres, and are excellently located, and are held by the Freedmen's Aid Society.

MORRISTOWN SEMINARY.

Our trip from Greensboro to Athens took us through Morristown and New Market, Tennessee. We have a good seminary in Morristown, well managed, and for which a building, costing twenty-five hundred dollars, is nearly finished. There are about one hundred and twenty-eight students here; three teachers; and the property is deeded to our Society.

Our school at New Market is for whites. The academy is small, and needs repairs. We are rendering aid to this school by paying the salary of one of the teachers.

EAST TENNESSEE WESLEYAN UNIVERSITY.

We visited next the institution for white students at Athens. There are in the college grounds about ten acres, on which is located a three-story brick building, which is used for chapel, recitation, and college purposes. They have commenced a brick church on the college grounds, and have laid the foundation, and are waiting for funds to complete it. There are about two hundred very promising students, gathered from all parts of that section of the South. We have rarely met a better appearing body of students; they are from the middle class of society, and are industriously laboring to prepare themselves for usefulness. There are six professors, industrious and doing good work. This institution is of great value to our work in that section of the country, and it has sent forth a large number of students qualified for teachers and preachers. Athens is a pleasant village, a quiet and moral place, and is a good location for a first-class institution, which will be needed here for many years to come.

HUNTSVILLE NORMAL SCHOOL.

We have in this place a normal school, with sixty-seven students in attendance, under the instruction of two teachers. We have nearly an acre of ground, and upon it a two-story brick building, with two recitation rooms on the first floor, and a school-room on the second. The State has established a normal school in the place, which interferes somewhat with the prosperity of our school. It has no accommodations for boarding students from abroad, and its patronage is mainly confined to the children of the town, and does not meet the object we have in view, of educating youth for teachers and preachers. This object can not be reached without securing a boarding-house and a large increase of expense, which, in view of the nearness of Nashville and Atlanta, where we have first-class institutions, we do not think it justifiable to make at present. The probability is, that at some future day we shall be compelled to do something more toward educational work in Alabama, and then it will be necessary to seek a more central and available location.

Thus we have visited our schools of the higher grade, and have not deemed it best to take the time and incur the expense of visiting several of our seminaries at places distant from our regular route. The Biblical Institute, at Baltimore, is one of the best of the institutions in our Southern work, but did not lie within the range of our present visitation. It has recently increased its faculty, and has entered upon a new era of interest in training young men for the ministry.

IMPRESSIONS.

1. We take pleasure in recording our satisfaction with the places selected for the location of our institutions. Each one of them is so located as to meet the wants of a large territory, and they are so related to each other that their lines of influence so meet as to form a net-work of educational agencies over a very large portion of the South. Even with the experience of the present hour, it would hardly be possible to locate these institutions more favorably. With the exception of Alabama, we have one of our higher institutions in each of the Southern States. In the selection of Little Rock, Arkansas, for the location of one of our universities, "to aid in the education of the white population," we have a position that commands the whole South-west, and when, at Chattanooga, Tennessee, our university for the South-

east shall be completed, we shall be able to meet all the wants for higher education in this part of our Southern work for years to come.

2. We supposed, when we started on this tour, that we should be able to see our way clear to recommend the reduction of the course of study in some of our colleges to a lower grade, and to concentrate the course of collegiate instruction within two or three of our leading institutions. But our observation has convinced us that this is not practicable. Our schools are far apart, and have been so located with reference to future needs, that it will be our wisest policy to develop one of these institutions in each State into a college proper. We do, however, think that in the present condition of this people, and in their present practical needs, they should not be urged to seek a complete classical education, but rather to become thorough in those practical English studies which will meet their immediate necessities. We should contemplate the establishment of no more colleges, with, perhaps, the exception of one in Alabama, at some future day.

3. We were much gratified by what we saw at Atlanta and Orangeburg of the movement inaugurated to give the students an opportunity of becoming acquainted with some kind of manual labor, by which they can obtain an honest livelihood without being entirely dependent upon their mental education. We believe this to be a wise movement, and, under the peculiar necessities of this people, should be encouraged in our schools.

4. We were disappointed in some of our institutions in not finding a larger number of students preparing for teaching and preaching, believing this to be the most important work to be accomplished in the schools in the present condition of our people. We therefore recommend that increased attention be given to such an education as will enable, as soon as possible, young men to go out into the work of the ministry, and others to enter the wide field of teaching their own people.

5. We were gratified to find in all our institutions a prevalent high tone of religion and morality, and that instruction was given in morals and good manners. We were impressed with the evidences of good order, politeness, cleanliness, and general good bearing among the students. Nearly all the schools have enjoyed revivals of religion during the year, and these are almost of annual occurrence.

6. We carefully examined the financial working of each of our institutions, and were impressed with the care and accuracy with which the accounts are kept, the carefulness and economy with which the expenditures are made, and the obvious concern of the officers to manage the interests intrusted to them as economically as possible. It is a matter of great congratulation that we have been enabled to establish and conduct so extensive an educational system on so small an expenditure of means.

7. It is a matter of devout thankfulness that the Church has been able in so short a time to establish so many schools of a high grade,

erect so many excellent and valuable buildings, to inaugurate so extensive a circle of educational forces, to educate so many youth, to accomplish so much in the elevation of a needy and oppressed people, and to disseminate so many and so great influences toward the improvement and advancement of so large a portion of our country.

8. We have been so deeply impressed with the great good accomplished by our schools in the South, and the imperative necessity for the permanence of this work, that we earnestly commend this Society to the liberality of our people, urge the pastors to raise large collections for it, and our men of wealth to endow professorships in these colleges, or to erect buildings for the schools suffering for accommodations, believing that no work in our land is more urgently demanded, and that none will render a richer or earlier harvest.

I. W. WILEY,
R. S. RUST.

THREE EPOCHS.

In the history of the negro in America there are three important epochs. The first embraces the foreign and domestic slave-trade. You are too familiar with the whole history of African slavery, beginning with the petty African princes making captives of the natives and selling them into hopeless bondage, to need a rehearsal of it. You understand the character of the passage from Africa to America; you are familiar with the horrors of the "middle passage." Thank God, the foreign slave-trade is broken up! Then followed and flourished the inter-State slave-trade. Such a trade was a burning disgrace to the nation. I never shall forget the sight, in Washington, I once saw, when a boy—a coffle of slaves—men and women chained together, marching through the streets, at the sound of a fife and drum, half famished, half-clad, poor, miserable wretches, going down into the perpetual bondage of the South. In a single year, authentic historians state, Virginia sent down into the far South forty thousand human beings, yielding a return of twenty-five million dollars! So disgraceful was this traffic that one of the Representatives in the Legislature of Virginia said: "Virginia is one grand menagerie, raising human beings, like oxen, for the shambles." Thank God that the nation is no more disgraced with that inhuman traffic—the inter-State slave-trade!

The next is the emancipation epoch; the toils, struggles, and triumphs of which are too fresh in your minds to need repetition. The emancipation of four millions of slaves was one of the grandest events ever recorded in history, and it awakened the loftiest notes of praise among the good both in heaven and earth.

The third epoch includes the reparation of the wrongs of the slaves, and the preparation of these millions of freedmen for Christian citizenship. Why did we emancipate the slaves? Why break up the traffic in human beings? Why annihilate the whole system of slavery, unless we educate the ex-slaves, unless we repair the wrongs we have inflicted on this people? Why strike the fetters from their limbs and leave their minds in the bonds of ignorance and degradation? In the language of Hon. Robert C. Winthrop: "Slavery is but half abolished, emancipation is but half completed, while millions of freemen with votes in their hands are left without education. Justice to them, the welfare of the States in which they live, the safety of the whole republic, the dignity of the elective franchise, alike demand that the still remaining bonds of ignorance shall be unloosed and broken, and the minds as well as the bodies of the emancipated go free."

Every argument for the overthrow of the slave-trade, both foreign and domestic, for the emancipation of the slaves, in thunder-tones demands for them education and elevation. The work of this third epoch is the most important of the three, and the struggles of the three center in this; therefore educate.

THE CENTENNIAL AND OUR SOUTHERN EDUCATIONAL WORK.

The year 1884 completes the first century of American Methodism. In order to recognize duly this important fact, the General Conference of 1880 recommended that the centennial of the Church be celebrated, and directed "that the matter be referred to the bishops to devise a plan for the centennial year, and report to the Church as early as convenient." In accordance with these instructions, the bishops submitted for the proposed celebration of its organization the following:

"*The chief object of connectional offerings should be the cause of education. The future of the Church will, under God's blessing, largely depend on the culture given to the youth. We commend to the liberality of the Church—first, the Board of Education; second, the Freedmen's Aid Society; third, Theological Schools; and fourth, such seminaries, colleges, and universities as shall be selected by the several annual conferences.*"

Through its constitution, as interpreted by the last General Conference, the Freedmen's Aid Society is responsible for our whole educational work in the Southern States, which now include nearly one-fourth of our entire membership.

The growth of our Church in the South is one of the marvels of modern ecclesiastical history. Here there has been a *net increase since* 1864 of fully three hundred thousand communicants, and of three thousand three hundred and eighty-five church buildings, valued at over six millions of dollars. Every argument which moved the Church to engage in the Southern work urges with increased intensity its vigorous prosecution.

It is greatly to the credit of our Church that she, through her Freedmen's Aid Society, is prosecuting with so much efficiency her educational work among the ignorant masses in the South, while the nation is discussing the dangerous illiteracy of this section, and yet hesitates to pass a bill to secure relief for educating the people.

The work of our Society has now reached a point where the demand for greatly increased financial aid becomes imperative. The days of Church primary schools in cabins are past. The public school system is undertaking, as it ought, this part of the work. The demand everywhere is for thoroughly educated preachers, well trained teachers, and for commodious and well furnished buildings. Our Society can not furnish schools for the vast number of illiterate youth in the South; it can only aid in the establishment of a few institutions of learning of a high grade for the preparation of preachers, teachers, and physicians, who, as leaders and educators, can give tone to public sentiment and aid in the dissemination of intelligence and religious truth. Our Church has never faced a graver responsibility than this, and only by a greatly enlarged outpouring of money can she meet this manifest call of God. During the centennial celebration each conference and congregation in the South will be encouraged to contribute as largely as possible to its local institutions. Already this spirit of self-helpfulness is apparent in several of the conferences.

The Society has expended three hundred and fifty thousand dollars in permanent school property. And yet every term hundreds of students are turned away from our schools for the want of accommodations. Our greatest need is new buildings at several important centers. One of these is New Orleans, where for years our school has suffered because of this want. In that commercial metropolis of the South, where Catholicism is so strongly intrenched, we have a Church membership and following of fully fifteen thousand, and within easy reach of this school are more than half a million negroes. Another point is Chattanooga, where, following the recommendation of the patronizing conferences, we have located our university for the Central South. With such a building as we need we could have an institution of commanding influence and largely self-supporting. Marshall, Austin, and Houston, Texas, and Orangeburg, South Carolina and Nashville, Tennessee, are other points at which buildings must be had, or the work will suffer greatly. We ought to have at least one hundred thousand dollars for new buildings during 1884.

Our next great need is endowments for professorships. Twenty thousand dollars will endow a chair. The salary of the president of each of our colleges should be secured by endowment. We also appeal for aid in educating young men and women. One thousand dollars will endow a perpetual scholarship, by which the donor could every year aid a worthy but poor young man or woman in obtaining an education.

We appeal to the Church for a centennial offering of at least two hundred and fifty thousand dollars in 1884. This would enable us to put one hundred thousand dollars into buildings, another hundred thousand into the endowment of professorships, and still enable us to support our schools without embarrassment.

We respectfully suggest:

1. That you heartily indorse, by special mention, our Southern educational work in your centennial appeal to the people, and urge our wealthy friends to remember this work in their centennial offerings.

2. We specially request every pastor, as early in the year as practicable, to deliver an address or sermon upon this subject, at which time the regular annual collection may be taken. Is it asking too much to request every pastor throughout our wide-spread connection to give at least one prominent service on the Sabbath to this cause, and that every congregation should be asked for a collection and every member for a donation?

3. In addition to our regular collections in the congregations our hope is largely in securing individual donations. Persons making donations can name the fund or the particular school to which they desire to contribute. We ask the pastors to call the attention of the benevolent and wealthy to this work—its large possibilities, and its pressing demands. Impress them with the fact that the centennial gifts to this cause will strengthen and establish the permanent agencies for the education and evangelization of those who have a peculiar claim upon the Church as well as the nation.

In behalf of the Society,

I. W. WILEY, *President,*
R. S. RUST, *Corresponding Secretary,*
J. C. HARTZELL, *Assistant Secretary,*
J. M. WALDEN, *Treasurer.*

REPORT OF AUDITING COMMITTEE.

CINCINNATI, *December* 1, 1883.

To the Executive Committee of the Freedmen's Aid Society:

BRETHREN,—We have made a careful and thorough examination of the accounts and vouchers of Dr. R. S. Rust, Corresponding Secretary of the Freedmen's Aid Society of the Methodist Episcopal Church, and also of the Treasurer, Dr. J. M. Walden, for the year ending July 1, 1883, and find the same correct and satisfactory. We have also canceled the vouchers of the Secretary.

A. SHINKLE.
JOHN J. HIGHT.

FINANCIAL STATEMENT.

The financial statement for the twelve months ending July 1, 1883, is as follows:

RECEIPTS FOR THE YEAR.

Cash in Treasury July 1, 1882,		$2,749 98
Contributed from July 1, 1882, to July 1, 1883,		106,077 09
Contributed by students in support of the schools,		12,076 63
Total,		$120,903 70
Loan to balance account,		21,635 90
		$142,539 60
Endowment of professorship in Gammon School of Theology, by Rev. E. H. Gammon,	$20,000 00	
Annuity—Rev. James H. Wilbur,	5,000 00	
Donations—Real estate at Oak Park, Ill., by Mrs. Adeline M. Smith, estimated at	10,000 00	
Michael Emeigh mortgage-note,	1,100 00	
		$36,100 00
Total,		$178,639 60
Collections from the Fall Conferences of 1882,	$33,463 09	
" " " Spring " " 1883,	30,209 24	
Received from Conference collections,	$63,672 33	
Received outside of Conference collections,	54,481 39	
	$118,153 72	
In Treasury July 1, 1882,	2,749 98	
	$120,903 70	
Loan,	21,635 90	
		$142,539 60
Endowment, annuity, and real estate,		36,100 00
Total,		$178,639 60

EXPENDITURES FOR THE YEAR.

Salaries and board of teachers and school expenses,	$58,433 95
Salary of Corresponding Secretary, office, and traveling expenses,	3,525 69
Salary of Assistant Secretary and traveling expenses,	3,507 37
Clerk hire,	900 00
Aid of young men for the ministry,	1,800 00
Interest on annuities,	2,890 00
Insurance and interest,	1,306 10
Furniture for schools,	1,290 26
Printing,	226 17
Repairs on buildings,	1,910 45
Postage,	172 15

Amount brought over, ... $75,962 14

ON REAL ESTATE AND BUILDINGS:

Clark University, Gammon Hall, Atlanta, Ga.,		$16,000 00
" " President's house, " "		1,200 00
" " land for Gammon Hall "		1,900 00
Cookman Institute, Jacksonville, Fla., ...		1,775 00
Houston Seminary, Houston, Texas, ...		3,500 00
Little Rock University, Little Rock, Ark., . .		18,500 00
Morristown Seminary, Morristown, Tenn., . .		1,500 00
Philander Smith College, Little Rock, Ark., .		8,000 00
Rust University, Holly Springs, Miss., ...		14,000 00
		$66,375 00
Total disbursements, July 1, 1883, ...		$142,337 14
Balance in Treasury, July 1, 1883, ...		202 46
		$142,539 60
Endowment, annuity, and real estate, ...		36,100 00
Total, ...		$178,639 60

Disbursed during sixteen years, ... $1,241,610 50

The Society has invested in permanent school property $450,000; 80,000 pupils have been taught in our institutions. Nearly a million of children have been taught by our teachers and by those prepared to teach in our schools.

The Society has received during the year $118,153.72; last year, $99,392.58—an increase of $18,761.14; and this increase in current receipts is from the following sources: Conference collections, $13,956.22; individual donations, $1,669.84; tuition and room rent for students, $3,135.08. It has expended, this year, $142,337.14; last year, $107,995.68—an increase in expenditures of $34,341.46.

The sum of $125,000 was apportioned by the Society as necessary to the prosecution of the work for the year; $118,153.72 was raised, leaving only a deficiency in that apportionment of $6,846.28. Amount of indebtedness incurred this year to balance account, $21,635.90; last year, $11,000—increase of incurred debt this year over last, $10,635.90. Amount expended in real estate and new buildings this year, $66,375; last year, $26,257.70—an increase of $40,117.30. This great advance in building has incurred the debt of $21,635.90.

Total receipts this year, $154,253.72; last year, $99,392.58; total increase, $54,861.14. Endowments, $36,100; receipts, $118,153.72—total receipts, $154,253.72; loan, $21,635.90; in treasury, July 1, 1882, $2,749.98; grand total, $178,639.60.

CONFERENCE COLLECTIONS, 1882.
Fall Conferences.

Conferences.	Amount.	No. Pastoral Charges.	No. taking Collections.	No. not taking Collections.	Amount per Member.	Apportionm't for 1883 and '84
1. Rock River	$3,579 11	200	179	21	.1167	$3,600 00
2. Cincinnati	3,217 89	144	136	8	.0881	3,600 00
3. North Ohio	2,334 96	124	108	16	.1000	2,500 00
4. Ohio	1,786 30	160	139	21	.0105	3,200 00
5. Illinois	1,782 05	211	164	47	.0492	2,500 00
6. Central Illinois	1,634 00	168	161	7	.0550	2,000 00
7. Central New York	1,620 00	204	176	28	.0549	3,000 00
8. East Ohio	1,537 79	195	182	13	.0347	3,500 00
9. Genesee	1,418 00	222	190	32	.0577	3,000 00
10. Central Ohio	1,403 72	125	109	16	.0548	2,500 00
11. Michigan	1,176 73	213	191	49	.0401	2,500 00
12. Upper Iowa	882 92	154	145	9	.0453	2,000 00
13. Pittsburg	831 00	143	104	39	.0255	2,600 00
14. Detroit	761 55	232	136	96	.0259	2,500 00
15. Erie	736 28	163	142	21	.0256	2,500 00
16. North-west Indiana	711 51	112	85	27	.0301	2,000 00
17. Minnesota	697 91	164	115	49	.0505	1,300 00
18. Wisconsin	642 21	142	113	29	.0521	1,300 00
19. Southern Illinois	557 28	127	117	10	.0226	1,100 00
20. Des Moines	528 16	151	118	33	.0239	1,300 00
21. Texas	518 35	68	56	12	.0597	300 00
22. South-east Indiana	492 24	89	81	8	.0197	1,800 00
23. Iowa	454 36	109	88	21	.0247	2,000 00
24. Kentucky	317 20	86	44	45	.0175	800 00
25. North-west Iowa	309 49	81	62	19	.0514	650 00
26. California	301 10	118	69	49	.0353	1,200 00
27. West Wisconsin	292 15	114	85	29	.0276	1,000 00
28. West Virginia	283 41	132	77	55	.0091	800 00
29. West Texas	279 81	60	40	20	.0130	300 00
30. Indiana	249 20	113	76	37	.0090	1,650 00
31. Central German	212 05	89	77	12	.0176	1,000 00
32. Savannah	210 95	88	59	29	.0197	600 00
33. Colorado	200 35	48	37	11	.0554	300 00
34. Nebraska	163 74	89	54	35	.0191	650 00
35. Tennessee	157 50	48	44	4	.0227	600 00
36. North-west Swedish	155 59	46	40	6	.0306	500 00
37. Columbia River	120 25	41	24	17	.0437	150 00
38. St. Louis German	113 65	87	68	19	.0136	600 00
39. Delaware	104 47	69	58	11	.0074	1,000 00
40. Oregon	86 10	52	24	28	.0109	650 00
41. Chicago German	79 00	57	45	12	.0139	800 00
42. North-west German	69 85	69	63	6	.0122	500 00
43. North-west Norwegian	58 25	34	25	9	.0247	100 00
44. Austin	49 45	23	12	11	.0538	150 00
45. Southern California	45 55	40	18	22	.0225	150 00
46. West German	45 20	46	26	20	.0132	300 00
47. East Tennessee	36 75	29	24	5	.0151	100 00
48. Central Alabama	31 00	48	24	24	.0048	150 00
49. Dakota Mission	29 90	32	8	24	.0139	25 00
50. Holston	27 70	60	32	28	.0016	600 00
51. Central Tennessee	27 05	49	31	18	.0056	500 00
52. North Nebraska	25 88	36	20	16	.0112	100 00
53. West Nebraska Mission	21 77	29	14	15	.0135	25 00
54. Nevada	15 25	24	4	20	.0217	150 00
55. Southern German	11 95	23	16	7	.0092	75 00
56. Montana Mission	5 50	11	2	9	.0121	75 00
57. Georgia	4 55	31	8	23	.0015	350 00
58. Alabama	1 10	24	2	22	.0002	150 00
59. Utah Mission		6		6		25 00
60. Black Hills Mission		7		7		25 00
61. New Mexico Mission		18		18		25 00
62. Arizona Mission		7		7		25 00
Total	$33,163 09	5,720	4,353	1,367		$69,650 00

CONFERENCE COLLECTIONS, 1883.
Spring Conferences.

CONFERENCES.	Amount.	No. Pastoral Charges.	No. taking Collections.	No. not taking Collections.	Amount per Member.	Apportionm't for 1883 and '84
1. New England	$3,633 00	222	154	68	.1219	$4,000 00
2. New York East	2,686 29	243	155	88	.0610	4,000 00
3. Philadelphia	2,637 09	233	210	23	.0581	1,000 00
4. Central Pennsylvania	2,157 16	181	176	5	.0513	3,200 00
5. New York	1,831 28	243	167	76	.0112	4,000 00
6. Louisiana	1,737 25	90	65	25	.1714	800 00
7. Baltimore	1,150 21	142	117	25	.0442	2,000 00
8. Troy	1,321 76	188	162	26	.0421	3,000 00
9. New Jersey	1,250 48	183	162	21	.0359	3,000 00
10. Newark	1,140 00	206	157	49	.0325	3,000 00
11. Wyoming	1,030 89	180	175	5	.0372	2,500 00
12. Mississippi	982 15	117	84	33	.0129	1,000 00
13. North Indiana	926 42	146	127	19	.0320	2,000 00
14. Northern New York	817 25	174	153	21	.0354	2,000 00
15. New England Southern	826 00	182	128	54	.0399	2,500 00
16. Washington	707 38	128	104	24	.0313	1,300 00
17. Wilmington	636 86	116	99	17	.0239	2,000 00
18. Vermont	631 91	163	131	32	.0412	800 00
19. New Hampshire	495 67	127	92	35	.0410	800 00
20. South Kansas	401 77	89	73	16	.0637	900 00
21. East Maine	387 00	102	75	27	.0433	650 00
22. Maine	378 08	110	82	28	.0348	800 00
23. Kansas	373 71	106	88	18	.0296	800 00
24. South-west Kansas	208 80	70	50	20	.0382	500 00
25. St. Louis	255 18	126	88	38	.0161	800 00
26. Missouri	243 70	120	84	36	.0141	650 00
27. Delaware	219 05	67	58	9	.0152	700 00
28. South Carolina	200 87	92	62	30	.0067	650 00
29. Lexington	152 34	106	55	51	.0217	500 00
30. East German	113 50	40	39	1	.0309	500 00
31. North-west Kansas	112 12	71	51	23	.0187	350 00
32. Little Rock	53 05	40	9	31	.0219	150 00
33. North Carolina	40 61	49	31	18	.0061	300 00
34. Florida	30 64	43	20	23	.0116	250 00
35. Arkansas	27 80	54	10	44	.0078	150 00
36. Virginia	17 31	45	19	26	.0029	150 00
37. Blue Ridge	4 33	24	10	14	.0009	50 00
Total	$30,209 24	4,621	3,522	1,099		$55,350 00
Spring Conferences ... 37	$30,209 24	4,621	3,522	1,099		$55,350 00
Fall Conferences ... 62	$33,463 09	5,720	4,353	1,367		$69,650 00
Grand Total ... 99	$63,672 33	10341	7,875	2,466		$125,000 00

Our ninety-nine Annual Conferences raised during the past year $63,672.33. The pastors of 2,466 charges neglected to take this collection—nearly one-fourth of the whole number. A contribution to this cause might be secured from almost every member of our Church and congregations, if the effort should be made by all our pastors. Will the pastors give the facts on this subject to the people, make a personal donation to it themselves in the public congregation, and urge their hearers to do likewise?

In behalf of the Board of Managers.

R. S. RUST, *Corresponding Secretary.*

December 5, 1883.

AMOUNTS RECEIVED

For the Year commencing July 1, 1882,

By REV. J. M. WALDEN, LL.D.,

Treasurer of the Methodist Freedmen's Aid Society.

July, 1882.

Carey, C. O. Con., by W. S. Paul	$15 00
Good Hope, C. Ill. Conference, by S. P. James	24 85
Dixon, Rock River Con., by O. F. Mattison	21 95
Rockford, Winnebago St. Church, R. R. Con., by W. H. Smith	17 00
Pontiac, C. Ill. Con., by E. Wusmuth	15 00
Whitewater, Wis. Con., by H. Sewell	6 00
Allen's Grove, Wis. Con., by T. Potter	2 00
Mazomanie, W. Wis. Con., by G. W. Nuzum	4 00
Cannon Falls, Minn. Con., by W. H. Soule	7 54
Reads and Wabasha, Minn. Con., by W. A. Miles	8 50
Minneapolis, Hennepin Ave., Minn. Con., by J. F. Chaffee	55 00
Anoka, Minn. Con., by H. G. Bilbie	15 00
Lake Crystal, Minn. Con., by G. F. Wells	5 00
Avoca, N. O. Con., by B. Hushour	7 20
Clyde, N. O. Con., by B. J. Hoadley	10 00
Darby, Mich. Con., by G. L. Mount	6 50
New Bloomfield, C. Penn. Con., by J. M. Johnston	15 00
Burbank, N. O. Con., by J. Whitworth	23 00
Buffalo, Ill. Con., by W. S. Calhoun	10 00
Saginaw, Washington Av., Detroit Con., by J. E. Springer	10 00
Augusta, Ky., Lexington Con., by A. McDade	3 26
Collections for Little Rock University, by Dr. Gray	147 60
Fair Haven and Sugar Valley, Cin. Con., by H. Witham	25 00
Orion, C. Ill. Con., by F. Doran	4 80
La Grange, Savannah Con., by Atlanta Depository	25 00
Plymouth, N. O. Con., by Dr. Rust	47 30
S. R. Parker, by Dr. Rust	500 00
Estate of Jesse Meharry, by Dr. Rust	2,197 00
Decatur, First Church and Strapp's Chapel, Ill. Con., by Bishop Warren	23 00
Kasson, Minn. Con., by A. Cressey	4 60
Hope, O. Con., by S. Rankin	10 00
Bequest of Mrs. Charlotte E. Howk, Wellington, O., J. W. Houghton, executor, by Dr. Rust	1,366 97
Lexington, Gunn's Chapel, Lexington Con., W. W. Locke, by D. Jones	10 00
Total	$4,943 07

August, 1882.

Sterling, Fourth St., R. R. Con., by J. Baum	$26 00
Hanover, R. R. Con., by H. M. Springer	8 40
Forreston, R. R. Con., by W. H. Strout	7 25
Chicago, Centenary Church, by A. C. George	56 00
Chicago, Western Ave., for Little Rock College, by J. H. Moore	27 50
Chicago, Halstead St. Church, by S. M. Davis	7 50
Peotone, R. R. Conference, by W. H. Hoadley	4 80
Panova, Des Moines Con., by J. W. Coe	10 00
De Soto, Des Moines Con., by D. Shenton	3 00
Mattawan, Mich. Con., by W. Jakways	4 50
Victor, Mich. Con., by G. Hollister	6 00
Big Rapids, Mich. Con., by E. S. Mechesney	10 00
Camden, Cin. Con., by G. T. Weaver	5 00
Mattoon, Ill. Con., by I. Villars	10 00
Woodbine Ct., Des Moines Con., by W. Douglass	5 00
Denver, Lawrence St. Church, Col. Con., by R. W. Manly	25 00
Gibson, Ill. Con., by J. Long	2 25
Parsons, S. Kan. Con., by H. Chaffee	8 00
Waverly, O. Con., by B. Thomas	5 00
Camargo, Ill. Con., by J. M. Goodspeed	35 00
Sarah Taylor, Lawrence, Mass., by Dr. Hartzell	1 00
Carrie A. Walker, Lawrence, Mass., by Dr. Hartzell	5 00
L. Beach, Jr., Lawrence, Mass., by Dr. Hartzell	10 00
A. R. Lunt, Lawrence, Mass., by Dr. Hartzell	10 00

R. W. Musgrove, Lawrence, Mass., by Dr. Hartzell	$1 00
Chicago, Grace Church, R. R. Con. (in part), by Dr. Hartzell	50 41
Syracuse University Church, N. Y. Con., by Dr. Hartzell	38 20
Syracuse, First Ward, N. Y. Con., by Dr. Hartzell	15 59
Syracuse, Centenary Church, N. Y. Con., by Dr. Hartzell	40 00
Shelbyville, Lex. Con., by S. Cottrell	2 00
Milton, Ind., S. E. Ind. Con., by D. Robertson	8 00
Mt. Auburn, Cin. Con., by J. Whetstone	30 00
"A friend," by John B. Hill	125 00
Morrow, Cin. Con., by V. F. Brown	9 50
Leesburg, Cin. Con., by J. Wilson	13 00
Franklin Furnace, O. Con., by P. Mark	20 00
Rising Sun, Ind., S. E. Ind. Con., by S. McMahan	3 00
Savoy, Ill. Con., by J. Kagey	5 00
Martinsville, Ind. Con., by J. Brant	7 00
Columbia, Cin. Con., by C. L. Conger	6 00
Hamilton and Mt. Pleasant, by J. Biers	1 35
Newport, Ky., C. Ger. Con., by J. Schaal	2 50
Louisville, Second Church, C. Ger. Con., by J. Barth	4 80
Jeffersonville, C. Ger. Con., by F. Hopp	5 00
Louisville, Market St., C. Ger. Con., by H. Lich	8 00
Casey, Ill. Con., by A. Graham	1 50
Bethel, Cin. Con., by F. Hypes	2 00
Mt. Lookout, Cin. Con., by E. T. Jane	7 00
Colorado Con. collections, by C. L. Libby	137 35
John Zacharius Lloyd, Roaring Creek, Penn. Con., to aid a colored young man in school, by Dr. Rust	24 72
S. E. Ind. Con. collections (additional), by Dr. Rust	482 49
Indianapolis, Grace Church, S. E. Ind Con., by Dr. Gray	8 55
Total	$1,350 46

September, 1882.

Lyndon, R. R. Con., by E. Brown	$3 35
Rockford Centennial, R. R. Con., by G. Vanhorn	58 20
Millington, R. R. Con., by H. Stoddard	6 00
Woodstock and Franklinville, R. R. Con., by J. Adams	20 50
Turner Junction, R. R. Con., by W H. Holmes	10 00
Evanston, First Church, R. R. Con., by T. C. Hoag	131 37
Orland, R. R. Con., by E. C. Arnold	15 00
La Mont, R. R. Con., by S. S. Snow	5 00
Newark, R. R. Con., by C. H. Hoffman	5 00
La Harpe, C. Ill., Con., by B. Applebee	1 75
Fisher, Ill. Con., by T. E. Madden	10 00
Jesup, Upper Iowa Con., by M. H. Smith	6 80
Fairfax, Upper Iowa Con., by N. E. Harmon	5 00
Cherokee, N. W. Iowa Con., by H. D. Brown	5 11
Dakota, N. W. Iowa Con., by J. Henderson	7 25
Spillsburg, W. Wis. Con., by T. Fullerton	7 00
Lancaster, W. Wis. Con., by C. Cook	10 00
Bloomington and Beetown, W. Wis., Con., by I. Le Baron	1 50
Monticello, W. Wis. Con., by R. Burnip	3 00
Oregon, W. Wis. Con., by J. Evans	7 15
Minneapolis, First Church, Minn. Con. by R. Forbes	20 00
Reeds and Wabash, Minn. Con., by W. A. Miles	2 00
Clearwater, Minn. Con., by L. B. Smith	2 00
N. W. Ind. Con. collections, by D. Morrison, treasurer	539 61
Pendleton, Cin. Con., by B. D. Hypes	5 00
Cincinnati, St. John's Church, Cin. Con., by W. E. Kugler	10 00
Delhi, Cin. Con., by C. W. Rishell	2 00
Hartwell, Cin. Con., by H. C. Wenkley	30 50
Avondale, Grace Church, Cin. Con., by J. P. Porter	25 00
Cheviot, Cin. Con., by J. S. Bitler	15 25
C. Ger. Con. collections, by H. C. Dickhaut	181 05
Cincinnati, York St. Church, Cin. Con., by F. G. Mitchell	35 00
Cincinnati, Wright's Chapel, Cin. Con., by C. H. Haines	5 00
Cincinnati, Mt. Auburn, Cin. Con., by J. H. Story	30 85
Lynchburg, Cin. Con., by M. P. Zink	11 00
Decatur Ct., Cin. Con., by S. W. Edmiston	11 10
Boston Ct., Cin. Con., by J. W. Sutherland	5 00
Cincinnati, McKendree Chapel, Cin. Con., by J. S. Whitney	3 65
Mt. Washington and Redbank, Cin. Con., by G. W. Dubois	2 50
Ripley, O., Cin. Con., by J. T. Bail	10 00
Madisonville, Cin. Con., by S. D. Clayton	28 70
West Virginia Con. collections, by J. Horner	9 00
Phillips and Hunt, by Dr. Rust	100 00
N. O. Con. collections, by P. F. Graham	951 08

TREASURER'S REPORT. 43

Clements, S. Ill. Con., by T. Eaton	$1 00
Jerseyville Station, S. Ill. Con., by E. May	10 00
Monticello, Ill. Con., by G. Alexander	2 25
Iowa Con. collections, by W. H. Smith	418 85
Ind. Con. collections, by J. Cooper	263 20
Chi. Con. collections, by W. B. Sellers	1,583 55
Bequest of Sarah Chapin, by F. Cox	281 25
Belvidere, Ill., First Ch., and Cherry Valley, R. R. Con., by A. Needham	5 00
Wheeling, Chapline St., W. V. Con., by J. Reed	15 00
I. O. Miles, Goshen, O., by Dr. Rust	3 00
C. O. Con., collections, by treasurer	755 07
Covington, Shinkle Chapel, Ky. Con., by S. G. Pollard	6 00
Nebraska Con. collections, by treasurer	161 50
Des Moines Con. collections, by treasurer	464 26
Ohio Con. collections, by G. B. Johnson	1,243 91
Armstrong, E. O. Con., by C. M. Hollett	5 00
Ill. Con. collections, by J. E. Artz	767 20
Southern Ill. Con. collections, by T. J. Massey	389 68
Ky. Con. collections, by A. Borcing	291 90
Clement Ct., S. Ill. Con., by T. A. Eaton	4 00
Carlyle, S. Ill. Con., by W. Wailis	3 00
Olney, S. Ill. Con., by J. W. Van Cleve	20 00
Miles Ct., S. Ill. Con., by N. H. Lee	7 00
Mt. Sterling Ct., Ill. Con., by R. Gregg	2 55
Vineland, St. Louis Con., by G. Dearborn	7 00
Harrisonville, St. Louis Con., by A. H. Parker	3 00
Davenport, St. Louis Ger. Con., by R. Tillman	1 00
Princeton, S. Kan. Cen., by R. T. Harkness	5 00
W. Nebraska Con., collections, by Dr. Fry	21 77
N. Nebraska Con., collections, by A. Hodgett	24 18
W. Ger. Con. collections by A. Bletch	40 20
St. Louis Ger. Con. collections, by H. C. Dickhaut	117 65
North-west Ger. Con. collections, by H. C. Dickhaut	61 85
Richmond, R. R. Con., by G. C. Clark	10 00
Erie, R. R. Con., by F. Lines	5 50
Wilmington, R. R. Con., by Wm. Clark	15 00
Ellwood, R. R. Con., by H. R. Antes	10 00
Chicago, Grand Place, R. R. Con., by L. Curts	20 00
Crete, R. R. Con. by G. M. Bassett	5 30
Meacham, R. R. Con., by T. E. Warrington	6 50
Waukegan, R. R. Con., by W. C. Dandy	14 00
McHenry, R. R. Con., by J. C. Bigelow	1 94
St. Charles, R. R. Con., by L. M. Hartley	7 75
Hanover, R. R. Con., by H. M. Springer	9 60
Oak Park, R. R. Con., by G. D. Esderkin	709 63
Sparland, C. Ill. Con., by R. Barton	5 00
Washburne, C. Ill. Con., by J. G. Blair	12 00
Lafayette, C. Ill. Con., by L. V. Webber	8 00
Blandinsville, C. Ill. Con., by C. Wayling	10 00
Piper City, C. Ill. Con., by L. Springer	4 50
Waverly, Upper Iowa Con., by J. C. Magee	5 25
Olin, Upper Iowa Con., by S. Goodsell	3 50
Decorah, Upper Iowa Con., by F. M. Robertson	8 00
Sargent Bluffs, North-west Iowa Con., by F. A. Burdick	8 00
Upper Iowa Con., collections, by W. Cummings	709 07
Fort Atkinson, Wis. Con., by J. D. Cole	2 00
Fond du Lac, Wis. Con., by S. Halsey	6 00
Evansville, Wis. Con., by H. Faville	4 00
Waukesha, Wis. Con., by P. W. Peterson	10 00
W. Wis. Con. collections, by treasurer	207 72
Chicago, First Church, North-west Swed. Con., by D. S. Sorlin	8 00
Chicago, Third Church, North-west Swedish Con., by J. Wigren	5 20
North-west Swedish Con. collections, by E. Shogren	131 65
Geneva and Batavia, North-west Swedish, Con., by S. Calendar	7 74
Total	$11,323 83

October, 1882.

Mich. Con. collections, by D. Casler	$615 12
North-west Iowa Con. collections, by St. Louis Depository	285 15
Chicago Ger. Con. collections, by treasurer	69 05
Steubenville, Lex. Con., by H. W. Tate	2 00
Lyons, C. N. Y. Con., by H. Cassavant	15 00
Legacy, John Pierce, deceased, by J. Proctor, executor	200 00
Blairstown, Newark Con., by E. Meacham	5 00
E. Tenn. Con. collections, by C. O. Fisher	31 95
Canon City Sunday-school, Colorado Con., by N. A. Chamberlain	25 00

Troy, O., Richards Church, Lex. Con., by J. Downs $1 25
Ironton, O., Lex. Con., by W. Heston 1 75
West Virginia Con. collections, by J. Horner 254 00
Pittsburg Con. collections, by J. Horner 777 52
Holston Con. collections, by W. P. Stowe 27 36

    Total $2,310 15

November, 1882.

Chicago, City Mission, R. R. Con., by W. C. Willing $11 00
  " Winter St. Church, R. R. Con., by W. Craven 11 00
  " Western Ave. Church, R. R. Con., by J. H. Moore 5 00
  " State St. Church, R. R. Con., by J. Richards 12 00
  " First Church, R. R. Con., by J. Williamson 105 00
  " St. Paul Church, R. R. Con., by J. Phelps 9 00
  " Wabash Ave. Church, R. R. Con., by F. Bristol 55 00
  " Michigan Ave. Church, R. R. Con., by M. Cady 51 50
Englewood, R. R. Con., by F. Hardin 6 00
Durand and Davis, R. R. Con., by W. Silberton 4 26
Rodgers Park, R. R. Con., by A. Yonker 2 00
Downer's Grove, R. R. Con., by A. Kistler 5 75
River Forest, R. R. Con., by J. M. Cost 6 00
Turner Junction, R. R. Con., by W. Holmes 7 82
Maple Rock and Dayton, R. R. Con., by J. W. Briggs 2 00
Willmette, R. R. Con., by J. Marlock 2 50
Mt. Carroll, R. R. Con., by C. W. Crail 22 00
Oak Park, R. R. Con., by G. Elderkin 28 00
Joliet, Richards St. Church, R. R. Con., by W. Tranter 10 00
Channahon, R. R. Con., by W. Minty 5 00
R. R. Con. collections, by G. Stuff 1,223 04
C. Ill. Con. collections, by T. Wood 775 51
Money Creek, by J. Stebbing 8 75
Minn. Con. collections, by J. Liscomb 541 08
Wis. Con. collections, by A. Porter 559 43
Dakota Mission collections, by F. Wheeler 29 00
Norwegian Mission collections, by A. Haagenson 18 25
Minn. Ann. collections, by Dr. Rust 31 00
Dr. R. S. Rust, for Bishop Warren's Training-school, by Bishop Warren. 10 00
Collections, by Dr. Hartzell 26 75
Rev. O. J. Squires, by Dr. Hartzell 5 00
Rev. J. S. Day, New England Con., bequest, by J. P. Magee 200 00
Hartford City, Ind., N. Ind. Con., by N. Gilliam 15 00
Dover, New Hampshire Con., by C. E. Hall 10 00
Richmond, N. Ind. Con., by F. Craft 20 00
New Zion, Lex. Con., by D. Jones 4 00
Marble Creek, Lex. Con., by D. Jones 2 00
Lorain, N. O. Con., by L. Markham 7 30
Phillips and Hunt, by Dr. Rust 6,000 00
Ladd annuity interest, by Dr. Rust 200 00
Eastman annuity interest by Dr. Rust 197 78
Wilbur annuity interest, by Dr. Rust 75 00
Hopkin's loan interest, by Dr. Rust 10 26
R. H. Robb, Atlanta, Ga., by Atlanta Depository 1 00
N. M. Alston, Savannah, Ga., by Atlanta Depository 5 00
C. O. Fisher, Atlanta, Ga., by Atlanta Depository 26 00
Dividend Eaton Bank stock, by Dr. Rust 16 23
Tenn. Conn. collections by treasurer 117 50
C. Tenn. Con. collections, by treasurer 25 00

    Total $10,561 61

December, 1882.

N. L. Carr, Flemingsburg, Ky., by Dr. Rust $5 00
Des Moines Con. collections (balance), by O. W. Blodgett 10 00
Mrs. D. H. Kramer, Carbondale, Kan., by Dr. Rust 5 00
Ill. Con. collections (balance), by J. B. Wolfe 4 00
Heyworth, Ill. Con., for Little Rock University, by Dr. Rust 5 00
F. M. Hayes, Clayton, Ill. Con., by Dr. Rust 2 80
Austin Con. collections, by A. A. Johnson 49 45
Winchester, Lex. Con., by F. Ross 6 00
North Middleton, Lex. Con., by J. Stanley 4 00
Georgetown, Lex. Con., by C. Nichols 1 00
Nancy Cathel estate, bequest, W. D. Burdett executor, by Dr. Rust 1,449 85
W. H. Evans, Lexington, Ky., by Dr. Rust 10 00
H. C. McDermitt, Factoryville, Penn., by Dr. Rust 13 00

De Witt, Upper Iowa Con., by G. Manning	$5 20
D. P. Hart, Tullahoma, Tenn., by Dr. Rust	25
Collections, Clifton Springs, N. Y., by Dr. Hartzell	236 60
Newton Wray, Wolcottville, Ind., by Dr. Rust	7 00
Mt. Washington and Redbank, Cin. Con., by G. W. Dubois	5 25
Georgia Con. collections, by Atlanta Depository	1 00
Savannah Con. collections, by Atlanta Depository	173 80
Alabama Con. collections, by Atlanta Depository	2 10
C. Ill. Con. collections, by Chicago Depository	5 00
Wis. Con. collections, by Chicago Depository	75
W. Wis. Con. collections, by Chicago Depository	7 22
Total	$2,012 33

January, 1883.

Sparta Ct. W. Wis. Con., by J. T. Morgan	$5 50
Rev. D. Handley, by Dr. Rust	10 00
Interest, Ladd Annuity, by Dr. Rust	200 00
Philo, Ill. Con., by R. Stephens	10 00
Seman Taber, Elwood, Kan., to educate a young man for the ministry, by Dr. Rust	25 00
Tolono, Ill. Con., by J. Dugan	8 85
Collections, by Dr. Hartzell	118 55
Huntsville, G. O. Con., by B. Herbert	7 35
Bloomington, Ind. Con., by J. E. Brant	6 50
Cincinnati, York St. Church, Cin. Con., by F. G. Mitchell	17 25
Cincinnati, Union Chapel, Lex. Con., by J. Moreland	5 00
T. B. Hopkins's Fund, Auburn, Cal., by Dr. Rust	174 75
Ada, C. O. Con., by A. C. Barnes	11 55
G. G. Cook, ex'tor of estate of Mrs. C. E. Hatch, Lowell, Mass., by Dr. Rust	250 00
Sundry contributions, by Dr. Rust	4 15
Total	$854 45

February, 1883.

Grand Ridge, C. Ill. Con., by O. Dunlevy	$11 00
Westfield, N. Ind. Con., by J. Cain	8 00
Montezuma, Iowa Con., by D. Smith	10 00
R. R. Con. collections (in part), by G. Elderkin	53 80
C. Ill. Con. collections (in part), by R. Brown	8 00
Iowa Con. collections (in part), by J. Barton	7 00
Des Moines Con. collections (in part), by D. Shenton	5 00
W. Wis. Con. collections (in part), by J. Holt	2 00
Cincinnati, Walnut Hills, Cin. Con., by Dr. Bayliss	70 00
Kossuth, Iowa Con., by O. Light	8 00
Washington, Kan. Con., by A. Watters	6 58
Garnett, S. Kan. Con., by F. Sisson	12 00
New Providence, Lex. Con., by D. Jones	2 00
Sharpsburg, Lex. Con., by G. Sissle	3 00
Phillips & Hunt, by Dr. Rust	953 78
South Whitley, Ind. Con., by F. A. Robinson	15 00
Washington, Wright's Chapel, Penn. Con., by Dr. Rust	3 00
Collections by Bishop Warren	300 00
La. Con., collections (in part), for Gilbert Haven School of Theology, by Dr. Hartzell	1,335 75
Rev. S. Osborne, New Orleans, by Dr. Hartzell	5 00
Rev. J. A. Dean, New Orleans, by Dr. Hartzell	30 00
Rev. S. Duncan, Shreveport, La., by Dr. Hartzell	25 00
J. Wilson, Mansfield, La., by Dr. Hartzell	5 00
Rev. A. E. O. Albert, New Orleans, by Dr. Hartzell	60 00
La. Con. Educational collections, turned over to F. Aid Society by vote of Con., by Dr. Hartzell	44 55
Morrow, O., Cin. Con., by V. Brown	8 00
Ligonier, N. Ind. Con., by J. Ervin	10 00
Miss. Con. collections (in part), by W. W. Hooper	1,000 00
Tex. Con. collections, by treasurer	685 00
Richmond, N. Ind. Con., by F. Craft	10 00
Con. collections, by J. P. Magee	305 01
Romeo, Mich. Con., by C. Morgan	10 00
Total	$5,011 47

March, 1883.

Waukegan, R. R. Con., by W. C. Dandy	$11 85
Sterling, Fourth St. Church, R. R. Con., by J. Baume	20 00

Galena, R. R. Con., by T. C. Clendenning	$10 00
Hampton, Upper Iowa Con., by C. McLean	10 00
Raymond, Upper Iowa Con., by S. C. Freer	6 50
Byron, Wis. Con., by J. E. Grant	2 80
Argyle, W. Wis. Con., by I. L. Baron	1 50
Osceola Mills, W. Wis. Con., by G. B. Russell	6 00
Cleveland, Scoville Ave., Erie Con., by D. H. Muller	22 00
Augusta, Ill. Con., by J. Wohlfaith	4 10
Centropolis, Kan. Con., by E. F. Holland	4 00
Butler, St. Louis Con., by T. Exly	5 00
Greenfield, St. Louis Con., by L. Wolfe	3 00
Holden, St. Louis Con., by C. J. Jones	8 25
Claremont, Mo. Con., by W. Van Gundy	5 00
Coffeyville, Kan. Con., by D. Summerville	4 00
S. Kan. Con. collections, by F. M. Sisson, treasurer	302 73
Cynthiana, Lex. Con., by G. Anderson	50
Cadentown, Ky., Lex. Con., by B. Studer	95
Collections by Dr Hartzell	391 56
Cincinnati, St. John Church, Cin. Con., by W. E. Kugler	17 10
Miss. Con. collections, by W. W. Hooper	718 50
Blanchester and Butlerville, Cin. Con., by J. McColm	7 08
Cincinnati, Walnut Hills, Cin. Con., by Dr. Bayliss	25 00
Rev. Jas. H. Wilbur, Columbia River Con., by Dr. Rust	105 00
Maysville, Lex. Con., by J. Courtney	10 00
Cincinnati, Union Chapel, Lex. Con., by J. Moreland	5 00
J. B. McCullough, Philadelphia, by Dr. Rust	270 00
Phila. Con. collections (in part), by Dr Rust	49 72
Wheeling, Chapline St., W. Va. Con., by J. Reed	15 00
Leesburg, Cin Con., by J. Wilson	12 00
Harlem Springs, E. O. Con., by M. Slutz	20 00
Augusta, Ky., Lex. Con., by A. McDade	1 74
Ironton, O., Lex. Con., by W. Hatton	25
Rev. E. H. Gammon, for Theological Seminary	2,000 00
S. W. Kan. Con. collections, by B. Swartz	249 75
St. Louis Con. collections, by F. Lenig	189 78
Springfield, Ill. Con., by G. Seringer	7 00
Bunker Hill, N. Ind. Con., by L. Naftzger	12 00
Champaign, Ill. Con., by I. Villars	10 00
Pittsburg, Pitts. Con., by C. Holmes	50 00
Belpre, O. Con., by J. Mitchell	6 00
Lex. Con. collections, by J. G. Jones	25
Cumminsville and Cheviot, Lex. Con., by W. Vaughn	2 00
College Hill, O., Lex. Con., by W. Vaughn	1 50
Portsmouth, O., Lex. Con., by W. Johnson	1 00
Mt. Pleasant Ct., Lex. Con., by W. H. Brown	2 00
Bellaire, O., Lex. Con., by R. Alexander	1 00
Springfield, O., Lex. Con., by W. Lankford	8 00
Dayton Mission, Lex. Con., by W. Echols	25
Paris, Ky., Lex. Con , by D. Jones	8 00
Washington, Ky., Lex. Con., by D. Jones	3 00
Germantown, Ky., Lex. Con., by B. Daniels	1 00
Phila. Con. collections, by Dr. Rust	1,573 56
Ausonia, C. O. Con., by P. Lemasters	4 30
Hardin, O., C. O. Con., by G. Matthews	9 45
St. Louis, Goode Ave. Church, St. Louis Con., by M. Wood	45
St. Louis, Water Tower Church, St. Louis Con., by J. Corrington	3 00
St. Louis, St. Luke's Church, St. Louis Con., by A. Jump	2 00
St. Louis, Union Church, St. Louis Con., by C. Felton	20 00
St. Louis Con. collections, by F. Lenig, treasurer	2 83
Mo. Con. collections, by J. G. Thompson	232 80
Gillespie Ct., S. Ill. Con., by J. Caldwell	5 00
Gibson City, Ill. Con., by T. Dillon	3 00
New Jersey Con. collections, by Dr. Rust	983 09
Betsey Cochran's estate, Romney, N. H., by B. Craig	300 00
Mt. Washington, Cin. Con., by G. DuBois	1 00
Lex. Con. collections, by treasurer	26 35
Oberlin, Rust Chapel, Lex. Con., by J. Hargrave	2 00
Mayslick and Lewisburg, Lex. Con., by J. Bowren	1 00
Collections for Gammon Hall, by Bishop Warren	4,000 00
Phillips & Hunt, by Dr. Rust	2,000 00
N. W. Kan. Con. collections, by Dr. Stowe	101 74
Lima and Van Buren, N. Ind. Con., by M. S. Marble	3 00
Thos. J. Davis, per son, W. O. Davis, New Jersey	20 00
R. F. Keeler, E. O. Con., by R. Munger	100 00
Total	$14,024 23

TREASURER'S REPORT. 47

April, 1883.

Sandwich, R. R. Con., by C. Thornton	$13 00
Minonk, C. Ill. Con., by T. Doney	12 00
Martinsville, Ill. Con., by A. McElfresh	6 00
Delmar, Upper Iowa Con., by J. M. Ferris	5 00
Clarence, Upper Iowa Con., by W. Chaffee	5 00
Janesville, Minn. Con., by F. H. Tubbs	2 00
Kan. Con. collections, by E. F. Hill	668 38
Medaryville, N. W. Ind. Con., by T. R. Faulkner	5 50
Amelia, O., Cin. Con., by H. C. Middleton	8 00
David Daily, by Dr Rust	20 00
Victor, Mich. Con., by G. Hollister	7 00
Keene, N. O. Con., by B. Hushour	8 30
Lebanon, Cin. Con., by D. C. Vance	20 00
Laramie City, Col. Con., by L. Hall	2 50
Hicksville, C. O. Con., by J. Simms	12 50
N. Ind. Con. collections, by Dr. Rust	818 42
East Berlin, N. Y. E. Con., by A. Loomis	2 00
Rutland, Vermont Con., by D. R. Lowell	10 00
J. L. Herron, E. O. Con., by R. B. Munger	100 00
Bakersville, N. O. Con., by F. McCauley	13 00
Sand Beach, Detroit Con., by G. Benedict	5 00
Brooklyn, Central Church, N. Y. E. Con., by Dr. Rust	13 51
Ansonia, C. O. Con., by P. Lemasters	3 13
Georgia Con. collections by Atlanta Depository	2 55
Collections for Gammon Hall, by Bishop Warren	2,000 00
Phillips & Hunt, by Dr. Rust	5,000 00
Newport, Grace Church, Ky. Con., by S. D. Watson	18 40
Total	$8,781 19

May, 1883.

Hopkins Fund, by Dr. Rust	$25 25
Byron, R. R. Con., by J. Hartman	5 00
Dixon, R. R. Con., by O. Mattison	20 00
Frankfort, R. R. Con., by John Roads	16 00
Lemont, R. R. Con., by J. T. Shaw	6 50
Newark, R. R. Con., by C. Hoffman	2 00
Grand Crossing, R. R. Con., by W. H. Holmes	13 50
Yorkville, R. R. Con, by E. W. Adams	21 50
Freedom, R. R. Con., by R. K. Bibbins	4 00
Monmouth, C. Ill. Conf., by R G. Pearce	25 00
Floyd, Upper Iowa Con., by C. Taylor	8 00
Central City, Upper Iowa Con., by T. M. Evans	13 00
St. Paul, Jackson St , Minn. Con., by W. K. Marshall	15 25
Collections, by J. A. Ruble	129 37
Niagara Falls, Genesee Con., by R. Copeland	11 00
Collections by Dr. Hartzell	1,000 00
New England Con. collections, by J. P. Magee	1,066 66
Southern New England Con. collections, by J. P. Magee	716 00
New Hampshire Con. collections, by J. P. Magee	391 30
Maine Con. collections, by J. P. Magee	326 08
Vermont Con. collections, by J. P. Magee	460 13
H. B. Palmer, Wakeman, O., by Dr. Rust	5 00
East Maine Con. collections, by J. P. Magee	285 00
Huntsville Normal School, tuition, by J. H. Owens	75 65
Dr. J. M. Ward, for Cookman Inst., by S. B. Darnell	50 00
Cook Howland, Ocean Grove, N. J., for Cookman Inst., by S. B. Darnell	5 00
Miss M. J. White, New York City, for Cookman Inst., by S. B. Darnell	10 00
Mrs. Martha Heston, Yardly, Penn., for Cookman Inst., by S. B. Darnell	25 00
Wm. Chandler, Wilmington, Del., for Cookman Inst., by S B. Darnell	10 00
Mrs. Eliza Meharry, Eaton, O., for Cookman Inst., by S. B. Darnell	500 00
Rev. J. E. Lake, Atlantic Highlands, N. J., for Cookman Inst., by S B. Darnell	50 00
Nathan H. Case, Ocean Grove, N. J., for Cookman Inst., by S. B. Darnell	100 00
W. F. Day, Morristown, N. J., for Cookman Inst., by S B. Darnell	5 00
Miss Hester Westerfield, Norwalk, Conn., for Cookman Inst., by S. B. Darnell	5 00
Chas. S. Bragg, Cincinnati, O., for Cookman Inst., by S. B. Darnell	10 00
J. M. Cornell, New York City, for Cookman Inst., by S. B. Darnell	5 00
R. Esterbrook, Camden, N. J., for Cookman Inst., by S. B. Darnell	3 00
J. M. Leeds, Germantown, Penn., for Cookman Inst., by S. B Darnell	5 00
Beulah Leeds, Germantown, Penn., for Cookman Inst., by S. B. Darnell	15 00
Wm. Matthews, Philadelphia, Penn., for Cookman Inst., by S. B. Darnell	100 00
Edw. Scally, Philadelphia, Penn., for Cookman Inst., by S. B. Darnell	5 00
S. Langford, Palmer, N. Y., for Cookman Inst., by S. B. Darnell	300 00

Thos. Kane, Chicago, Ill., for Cookman Inst., by S. B. Darnell	$30 00
J. W. Fitzgerald, Baltimore, Md., for Cookman Inst., by S. B. Darnell	5 00
A. S. Barnes, New York City, for Cookman Inst., by S. B. Darnell	10 00
B. U. Paine, Corning, N. Y., for Cookman Inst., by S. B. Darnell	10 00
Collections by Hattie Morehouse, Newark, N. J., for Cookman Inst., by S. B. Darnell	6 80
Rev. J. F. Lake, N. J., for Cookman Inst., by S. B. Darnell	85 00
Rev. J. Brien, Southold, L. I., for Cookman Inst., by S. B. Darnell	20 00
T. U. Lillayne, Ocean Grove, N. J., for Cookman Inst., by S. B. Darnell	45 00
Miss Laura Stevens, Ocean Grove, N. J., for Cookm'n Inst., by S. B. Darnell	45 00
Miss Sallie Leeds, Germantown, Pa., for Cookman Inst., by S. B. Darnell	45 00
Mrs. F. W. Owen, Morristown, N. J., for Cookman Inst., by S. B. Darnell	105 50
Isaac Beale, Asbury Park, N. J., for Cookman Inst., by S. B. Darnell	45 00
Mrs. J. Knapp, Brooklyn, N. Y., for Cookman Inst., by S. B. Darnell	25 00
Small donations for Cookman Inst., by S. B. Darnell	5 25
Cookman Inst., tuition and room-rent, by S. B. Darnell	274 00
Bennett Seminary, tuition, room-rent, and incidentals, by W. F. Steele	588 56
Cash from a friend, for Bennett Seminary, by W. F. Steele	70 00
J. McNab, for Bennett Seminary, by W. F. Steele	1 00
Mrs. D. Steele, for Bennett Seminary, by W. F. Steele	5 00
Friends, Boston St., M. E. Sunday-school, Lynn, Mass., for Bennett Seminary, by W. F. Steele	20 00
E. Taylor and wife, for Bennett Seminary, by W. F. Steele	15 00
Friends, Edgartown, Mass., M. E. Church, for Bennett Seminary, by W. F. Steele	13 09
Special colls. at Cottage City, Mass., for Bennett Seminary by W. F. Steele	76 00
Wm. H. Phillips and wife, for Bennett Seminary, by W. F. Steele	132 00
Cyrus Washburn, for Bennett Seminary, by W. F. Steele	25 00
Friends, per Adelia Hall, for Bennett Seminary, by W. F. Steele	50 00
Friends at St. Paul M. E. Church, Lynn, Mass., for Bennett Seminary, by W. F. Steele	25 00
Miss A. M. Hall, for Bennett Seminary, by W. F. Steele	35 00
Friends, per Adelia Hall, for Bennett Seminary, by W. F. Steele	15 00
S. C. Hathaway, for Bennett Seminary, by W. F. Steele	50 00
P. Sims, for Bennett Seminary, by W. F. Steele	35 00
H. W. Gilman, for Bennett Seminary, by W. F. Steele	35 00
D. Steele, for Bennett Seminary, by W. F. Steele	35 00
Friends at Peabody (Mass.) M. E. Church, for Bennett Seminary, by W. F. Steele	41 50
Mrs. J. M. Woods, for Bennett Seminary, by W. F. Steele	15 00
L. M. Leach, for Bennett Seminary, by W. F. Steele	25 00
Camden, N. J., by Dr. Rust	1 00
Eaton National Bank, interest, by Dr. Rust	23 76
M. A. Kinnear, Kingsville, O., by Dr. Rust	5 00
L. T. Willsee, C. O. Con., Toledo, O., by Dr. Rust	12 50
State of South Carolina, for Claflin University, by Dr. Cooke	5,000 00
Claflin University, room-rent, by Dr. Cooke	1,026 82
" " Farm products, by Dr. Cooke	750 00
" " Incidentals, by Dr. Cooke	589 10
" " Peabody Fund, by Dr. Cooke	500 00
" " Educational Society, by Dr. Cooke	150 00
Soc. for Prop. the Gospel for Claflin University, by Dr. Cooke	200 00
W. H. M. Society, for Claflin University, by Dr. Cooke	85 00
Hon. A. A. Lawrence, Boston, Mass., for Claflin Univ., by Dr. Cooke	125 00
C. Meinam, Esq., Springfield, Mass., for Claflin Univ., by Dr. Cooke	50 00
Rev. W. F. Whittaker, Lowell, Mass., for Claflin Univ., by Dr. Cooke	26 00
Mrs. C. Davis, Lowell, Mass., for Claflin Univ., by Dr. Cooke	25 00
J. A. Woolson, Esq., Boston, Mass., for Claflin Univ., by Dr. Cooke	21 00
Rev. A. C. Dutton, Vineland, N. J., for Claflin Univ., by Dr. Cooke	15 00
J. Y. Kreps, Esq., for Claflin Univ., by Dr. Cooke	15 00
Mrs. Geddings, California, for Claflin Univ., by Dr. Cooke	10 00
Misses H. and L. Fish, Natick, Mass., for Claflin Univ., by Dr. Cooke	10 00
Mr. Stearns, Newton, Mass., for Claflin Univ., by Dr. Cooke	2 00
Will of Cath. McCaskey, La Porte, Ind., by Dr. Rust	21 50
J. Nikes, Sylvania, C. O. Con., by Dr. Rust	12 25
W. J. Barger, Carleton, Neb. Con., by Dr. Rust	10 00
Romulus, Detroit Con., by I. Goodson	3 16
Taylor, Detroit Con., by I. Goodson	2 13
Sand Hill, Detroit Con., by I. Goodson	1 26
Sundry collections, Detroit Con., by I. Goodson	3 45
Toledo, C. Ger. Con., by C. Bozenhat	2 00
Morristown, North-west Ger. Con., by D. Pfaff	2 00
Berea, N. O. Con., by A. Y. Lyon	13 20
New England colls. for Gilbert Haven Theol. School, by Dr. Hartzell	400 00
Lockland, Cin. Con., by A. Bowers	21 00
D. M. Clayton, B. R. Avery's Creek, N C., by Dr. Rust	4 00
Rev. O. Upsher, for Morristown Seminary, by J. S. Hill	20 50
Morristown Dist. Con., E. T. Con., for Morristown Sem., by J. S. Hill	4 10

TREASURER'S REPORT. 49

E. Tenn. Con. Ed. Meeting, for Morristown Sem., by J. S. Hill	$37 25
Brown, Wells & Hoyt, for Morristown Sem., by J. S. Hill	15 25
Camden, 3d St. Church, N. J. Con., for Morristown Sem., by J. S. Hill	16 00
Trenton, C. Church, N. J. Con., for Morristown Sem., by J. S. Hill	20 00
Trenton, Ham. Ave. Church, for Morristown Sem., by J. S. Hill	10 00
L. Parker, Trenton, N. J., for Morristown Sem., by J. S. Hill	5 00
C. P. Smith, Trenton, N. J., for Morristown Sem., by J. S. Hill	5 00
Rev. J. R. Mace, Trenton, N. J., for Morristown Sem., by J. S. Hill	5 00
John Moser, Trenton, N. J., for Morristown Sem., by J. S. Hill	25 00
Cambridgeport, Mass., Green St. Ch., for Morristown Sem., by J. S. Hill	10 00
" " Howard St. Ch., for Morristown Sem., by J. S. Hill	10 00
Phila., Tabernacle Ch., for Morristown Sem., by J. S. Hill	85 00
Brunswick, Pitman Ch., N. J. Con., for Morristown Sem., by J. S. Hill	4 18
Phila., 12th St. Ch., for Morristown Sem., by J. S. Hill	19 00
Phila., 19th St. Ch., for Morristown Sem., by J. S. Hill	15 00
Camden, Tabernacle Ch., N. J. Con., for Morristown Sem., by J. S. Hill	30 00
Trenton, N. J., Hon. A. J. Whittaker, for Morristown Sem., by J. S. Hill	20 00
Charles Scott, Phila., for Morristown Sem., by J. S. Hill	25 00
Mrs. C. Boyd, " " " " " "	25 00
Wm. Boswell, Trenton, N. J., for Morristown Sem., by J. S. Hill	5 00
A. H. Gregg, Morristown, Tenn., for Morristown Sem., by J. S. Hill	25 00
Miss Kate Weeks and pupils, Trenton, N. J., for Morristown Sem., by J. S. Hill	5 15
Camden, Broadway Ch., N. J Con., for Morristown Sem., by J. S. Hill	27 00
Ashland, Mass., N. Eng. Con., for Morristown Sem., by J. S. Hill	4 00
Natick, " " " " " "	25 00
Boston, Temple St. Ch., N. Eng. Con., for Morristown Sem., by J. S. Hill	6 57
Rev. A. Howard, N. Y. City, for Morristown Sem., by J. S. Hill	5 00
J. H. Frey, Baltimore, Md., for Morristown Sem., by J. S. Hill	30 00
Cambridgeport, Howard St. Ch., N. Eng. Con., for Morristown Sem., by J. S. Hill	32 00
Various contributions for Morristown Sem., by J. S. Hill	16 13
Total	$18,341 75

June, 1883.

Central Illinois Conference:	
Verona, by Rev. C. Green	$10 00
Central Tennessee Conference:	
Spruce St., Nashville, by Rev. V. Randolph	4 50
Colorado Conference:	
Lawrence St., by Rev. R. W. Manley	40 00
Georgetown, by Rev. C. L. Libby	7 00
Lexington Conference:	
Lands, Ky., by Rev. D. Hickman	50
Winchester, by Rev. W. W. Locke	11 00
Flemingsburg, Ky., by Rev. H. Southgate	6 00
New Zion, Ky., by Rev. J. Stanley	6 00
N. Middletown, Ky., by Rev. F. Ross	3 00
Washington, Ky., by Rev. C. J. Nichols	1 00
Minnesota Conference:	
Anoka, by Rev. H. Bilbie	12 00
Cannon River Falls, by Rev. W. Soule	8 20
Stillwater, by Rev. T. McClary	11 00
Nebraska Conference:	
Falls City, by Rev. J. Gallagher	4 00
North Ohio Conference:	
Tiffin, by Rev. J. S. Reager	27 00
Wooster, by Rev. N. Albright	27 25
Ohio Conference:	
Roseville, by Rev. I. Sollars	15 00
Claysville, by Rev. J. Starkey	45 00
Rock River Conference:	
Elwood, by Rev. H. Antes	15 00
Thompson, by Rev. Thos. Cochran	4 25
Plainfield, by Rev. E. C. Arnold	14 00
Fulton, by Rev. E. S. Holm	7 40
Batavia, by Rev. N. Freeman	18 00
Bethel, by Rev. A. Miller	12 05
Apple River, by Rev. O. Burch	8 00
South Illinois Conference:	
Wakefield Circuit, by Rev. J. Jackson	10 40
Clement Circuit, by Rev. T. Eaton	4 00
Tamaroa, by Rev. J. R. Reef	10 00
South Kansas Conference:	
Parsons, by Rev. H. W. Chaffee	9 50
Cherryvale, by Rev. C. Durboraw	5 58

4

South-west Kansas Conference:
Binden, by Rev. T. Shelton	$10 00
Central Tenn. College, Tuition, by Dr. Braden	2,128 00
" " " Room-rent, by Dr. Braden	1,166 15
" " " Farm in Indiana, by Dr. Braden	496 30
" " " Miss L. Battle, by Dr. Braden	50 00
" " " H. Blythe, by Dr. Braden	28 80
" " " W. C. DePauw, by Dr. Braden	100 00
" " " Rev. H. Deiner, by Dr. Braden	25 00
" " " Rev. B. Kephart, by Dr. Braden	30 00
" " " Rev. Jesse Durbin, by Dr. Braden	30 00
" " " Educational Society, by Dr. Braden	140 00
" " " J. C. O'Kane, by Dr. Braden	30 00
" " " J. V. Webster, by Dr. Braden	70 00
" " " R. S. Rust, by Dr. Braden	15 00
" " " Mrs. F. A. Meharry, for Med. Col., by Dr. Braden	600 00
" " " Rev. S. Meharry, for Medical Col., by Dr. Braden	130 00
" " " Dr. Meharry, for Medical College, by Dr. Braden	30 00
" " " W. Patterson, for Medical College, by Dr. Braden	30 00
" " " G. W. Hubbard, for Medical Col., by Dr. Braden	50 00
" " " Various donations for Med. Col., by Dr Braden	75 75
New Orleans University, tuition, by Dr. Dean	968 45
Fleet St. Church, Brooklyn, by Dr. Dean	25 00
Mystic Bridge, New Eng. Con., by Dr. Dean	15 00
New London, New Eng. Con., by Dr. Dean	11 00
Various contributions, by Dr. Dean	35 15
Dr. Jas. A. Dean, by Dr. Dean	4 10
Central Biblical Institute:	
Baltimore Con. collections, by Dr. Frysinger	1,152 21
Wilmington Con. collections, by Dr. Frysinger	612 87
Washington Con. collections, by Dr. Frysinger	726 02
Personal donations, by Dr. Frysinger	1,118 71
Tuition, by Dr. Frysinger	519 92
Walden Sem., tuition, by F. Mason	322 45
La Grange Sem., tuition, by O. D. Wagner	170 75
Clark University, by E. O. Thayer:	
H. K. List	50 00
Cash, by Bishop Warren	10 00
E. O. Fisk	450 00
Hon. P. Sawyer	25 00
Rev. H. Sewall	12 00
Rev. Mr. Wilson	11 50
Rev. C. H. Heard	33 00
Appleton, Wis., Friends	28 50
Miss Jane Bancroft	70 00
Wellesley College	20 00
Gayton Ballard	200 00
Miss Carrie Allen	7 00
Missionary Society, Kent's Hill, Me	14 15
East Tauas Church, Mich	20 65
Mrs. L. B. Smith	2 50
Mrs. D. J. Knox	5 00
C. Davenport	5 00
Mrs. S. P. Robie	2 00
Miss E. Folwell	5 00
C. P. Nixon	5 00
Mrs. Harrison	27 00
E. H. Gammon	5 00
Mrs. D. J. Knox	45 00
Ladies of Appleton, Wis	51 00
Mrs. Frank Felt	27 00
Mrs. H. G. Ladd	30 00
Hon. H. K. Braley	100 00
Harper & Bros	25 00
Walden & Stowe	15 00
A friend	5 00
B L. Boorner	10 00
Judge Reynolds	10 00
W. W. Thayer	10 00
S. A Corney	10 00
J. W. Wellman	5 00
Rev. F. Otheman	10 00
Rev. L. R. Thayer	10 00
H. O. Houghton	10 00
Hon. J. Sleeper	25 00
Milton Bradley	10 00
Z. T. Spencer	18 00
Additional collections, by J. S. Hill	7 33

TREASURER'S REPORT.

Collections for Gammon Hall, by Bishop Warren	$3,500 00
Collections for Gammon Hall, by Bishop Warren	2,500 00
Rev. E. H. Gammon, for Theological Hall, by Dr. Rust	2,000 00
Morristown Seminary, tuition and incidentals, by J. S. Hill	484 49
Wiley University, tuition and room-rent, by W. H. Davis	1,289 47
Rust University, tuition and room-rent, by W. W. Hooper	1,654 88
Clark University, tuition and room-rent, by E. O. Thayer	1,082 35
Collections by Dr. Hartzell	1,000 00
Collections for Little Rock University, by Dr. Gray	7,284 50
Houston Seminary, tuition, by C. Campbell	386 56
Collections by Dr. Hartzell	1,292 23
Estate of Catherine McCaskey, La Porte, Ind., by trustees M. E. Church	15 50
Bequest, Kinsey note, by Dr. Rust	1,272 81
Bequest, Kinsey note, by Dr. Rust	602 00
Whitehall St. property (in part)	1,600 00
Meridian Academy, tuition, by Mrs. M. V. Keever	419 50
Total	$38,639 18

SUMMARY.

1882—	July,	$4,943 07
	August,	1,350 46
	September,	11,323 83
	October,	2,310 15
	November,	10,561 61
	December,	2,012 33
1883—	January,	854 45
	February,	5,011 47
	March,	14,024 23
	April,	8,781 19
	May,	18,341 75
	June,	38,639 18
	Grand Total,	$118,153 72

SUMMARY OF ANNUAL DISBURSEMENTS.

First	Year, total disbursements,		$37,139 89
Second	" " "		50,167 24
Third	" " "		*93,513 50
Fourth	" " "		*82,719 49
Fifth	" " "		51,568 43
Sixth	" " "		55,134 98
Seventh	" " "		66,995 74
Eighth	" " "		86,562 88
Ninth	" " "		58,204 75
Tenth	" " "		70,442 65
Eleventh	" " "		63,402 85
Twelfth	" " "		75,260 76
Thirteenth	" " "		104,376 25
Fourteenth	" " "		95,788 27
Fifteenth	" " "		107,995 68
Sixteenth	" " "		142,337 14

Amount collected and disbursed during Sixteen years, $1,241,610 50

* Including appropriations from Freedmen's Bureau.

ANNIVERSARY

OF THE

FREEDMEN'S AID SOCIETY.

The Sixteenth Anniversary of this Society was held in the auditorium at Ocean Grove, New Jersey, August 13, 1883. Rev. Dr. J. A. DEAN, President of New Orleans University, offered the opening prayer.

Bishop HARRIS presided during the three sessions, morning, afternoon, and evening, and added greatly to the interest of the anniversary by his words of wisdom and encouragement.

The Corresponding Secretary, Dr. R. S. RUST, presented an abstract of the Annual Report of the Treasurer and the Board of Managers, which will be found in the preceding report.

OUR SCHOOL WORK.

By PROF. W. H. CROGMAN, A. M.,
CLARK UNIVERSITY, ATLANTA, GA.

I AM indebted to my good and venerable friend, Dr. Rust, for the privilege I have to-day of speaking here on the breezy shores of Ocean Grove, on topics relating to my people down in that sunny section of country which they so largely inhabit; and it shall be my endeavor, in the short time allotted me, to confine myself to a consideration of the work done among this people by the Christian Church in general, by the branch of it to which I belong in particular, and to show that this work has not been done in vain, that it has been productive not only of results, but of results as salutary as to many they have been surprising. From these considerations I shall hope to convince you that the Negro to-day, more than ever, is entitled to your confidence, your esteem, your sympathy, your generous aid, and hearty co-operation.

Unlike the traducers of my race, I shall endeavor to do this by telling the truth, by appealing to facts, sharp, clean, clear-cut, unerring facts; facts which somehow always make havoc of fancies, facts which malice can not obscure nor prejudice controvert. Neither, indeed, would it be wise in me to attempt any thing but a fair representation of my race while surrounded by so many good and honored men who are perfectly acquainted with that Southern work, even in its minor details; men, too, not only of my own denomination, but of the various denominations who have come up here to celebrate with us, and whose presence is to me one of the happiest features of this occasion. For it is, to say the least, beautifully illustrative of the fact, that however much we may differ in our religious views, and however much we may at times even bicker over these little denominational differences, yet beneath and beyond all this there is a strong cord of sympathy and love running through and connecting the hearts of our common Protestantism. We are one—one in our aims, one in our efforts, and nowhere; perhaps, in these latter days, has this unity of purpose and action on the part of the various branches of the Christian Church been more clearly shown than on the Southern field in the work among the freedmen.

At the close of the war, and I may well say before the close of the war, a perfect crusade was made southward, a crusade, indeed, but little resembling those of the olden time. Unlike those, its numbers were small, and did not come just as Heber tells us in his splendid verse the ancient crusaders came,

"With their limbs all iron, and their souls all flame."

No. The defensive armor of our modern crusaders was a "heart untainted" and fully conscious of having its "quarrel just." Their weapons, too, were neither the sword nor the battle-ax, but the Bible and the spelling-book. With these they entered the field—Unitarian and Orthodox, Baptists, Methodists, Presbyterians, Congregationalists—all shoulder to shoulder, side by side, and with a zeal, a courage, and a devotion hardly surpassed in the history of the Church, began the new conflict against the more deadly enemies of the republic, ignorance and vice, mother and child.

No field on the face of God's earth was at that time less inviting. Cruel war had hardly yet closed his bloody mouth, and the South, writhing under a wounded pride, and the heavy losses sustained in property, was, as could only be expected, bitterly hostile to Negro education, and to all who engaged in it in any way, shape, or form.

To be deprived of their Negroes was considered bad enough, but to see those same Negroes seated in the school-room, and acquiring that very education which had been prohibited by law under heavy penalties, was simply intolerable. Hence it is easy to account for the burning of so many school-houses, and the cruel and brutal treatment of so many Northern teachers during those early days of reconstruction. Indeed, even now, after a lapse of eighteen years—within which time, it must be frankly acknowledged, Southern sentiment has undergone quite a change, and the better classes of the Southern people have come to recognize the necessity of universal education to the welfare of society—even now, I say, the teacher of the Negro does not everywhere meet that warm-hearted hospitality which, with reason, he ought to expect, and which has always been so proverbially attributed to the Southern people.

In marked contrast, however, with the enmity of the whites was the friendliness of the blacks. These poor, ragged, hungry, homeless creatures greeted everywhere with joy and gladness their new benefactors, submitted themselves to their instruction and guidance, and in many instances even periled their own lives in their behalf. Rev. T. Willard Lewis, a most estimable man, but long since passed to his reward, while organizing in South Carolina the work of the Methodist Episcopal Church, was several times attacked by armed ruffians, and as many times escaped only through the prompt and manly intervention of his black friends.

Rev. George Standing, of the same Church, an Englishman, who came to this country at the close of the war, for the purpose of laboring among the freedmen, went to Newnan, Georgia, his field of labor, expecting, as he said, to be most cordially welcomed. To his bitter disappointment, however, on arriving there he found that even the very storekeepers were a unit against selling him food to eat. It was but a few years ago, when, in a sermon referring to those gloomy days, I heard him exclaim, while the tears glistened in his eyes, "Yes, when thirteen years ago I went to Newnan the white people tried to starve me out, and when, for neither love nor money, I could purchase a bit of meat on their streets to satisfy my hunger, a good old colored brother would take his gun upon his shoulder and go into the woods and hunt rabbits to feed me."

These are but a few cases in this line which I might mention. I refer to them, friends, simply to show, that while you out of your abundance have been faithful to us, out of our poverty we have been faithful to you.

But there were other things besides ostracism and open violence to discourage the early missionaries and to try their faith. The very materials out of which they were to build up manhood were considered by most people North, as well as South, to be of a very doubtful nature. In the South, the home of the Negro's degradation, he was, of necessity, looked upon as an inferior being, incapable of education, and only fitted to be a chattel. The same idea had, to large extent, taken possession of the Northern mind, and more strongly, too, I think. For while it is true that the people of the North were far removed from the scenes of slavery, and came not into contact with the large masses of the blacks, yet there were in the midst of Northern society forces and influences continually at work misrepresenting the Negro.

The newspapers, with but few exceptions, had been accustomed to speak of him in any thing but a kindly and respectful manner. Some of these wretched sheets have hardly yet repented of their sins. Science, in many instances, had traced his origin back to the monkey; and, even now, there can be found a few who are but little in advance of that jackanapes theory, a few who seem to take real delight in raking over the *debris* of the pre-adamitic world to prove that the Negro did not spring from the same progenitors with yourselves and the other races of the earth. Art, too, lent its fascinating, but mischievous, pencil to paint him in form and features the most repulsive. Every colored person was represented with flat nose, thick lips, long heels, and dressed in a striped suit, the well-known garb of the American slave. Such was his picture in the cotton-field and in the canebrake, and such was the picture which the manufacturers of shoe-blacking and stove-polish deemed most appropriate to accompany the labels on their boxes of goods. Mothers and nurses were accustomed to frighten peevish children to sleep by telling them that the black man should come and take them. The black man, forsooth, some hideous monster! The injustice of all this has become apparent since the war. Northern people traveling through the South have discovered that we are not so bad looking after all; that many of us, indeed, just like other people, when we are cleaned up and brushed up and dressed up and behave ourselves, are really pretty good looking. Fine feathers make fine birds; but, in all ages, the tattered garments of slavery have been but ill adapted to set off to best advantage the forms and features of mankind. I say it, and I say it without fear of successful contradiction, that many of the handsomest citizens the United States can boast of to-day have the warm blood of Africa coursing through their veins. We are black, but comely; and we are not so black either; for, surely, of all perplexing things, the most perplexing to strangers traveling through the South to-day is the great diversity of shades and colors among the population called the Negro population. These range all the way from black to dark brown, to brown, to light brown, to yellow, to light yellow—and so on all the way up to the fair-haired and the blue-eyed, where shades have been so blended and inter-blended, and the dividing line so completely obliterated, that it is hard to tell where Ham left off and Japhet began.

But to return, for I was speaking of the pro-slavery influences at work among the people of the North, before the war, to prejudice their minds against the Negro. I have alluded to the attitude of the press, of science, of art; to which must be added that crowning iniquity—I mean those bands of vile men, commonly known as "nigger minstrels," who, traveling all over this broad country, caricatured the negro upon the public stage before large and enthusiastic audiences. The result of these influences combined was the creation in the Northern mind of an *ideal* Negro which, in many respects, was even more degraded than the real Negro of the South.

Such, then, was the field, and such the doubts, the shadows, the misgivings which enveloped it when Christian faith and charity came to the rescue.

What are the facts to-day? Within the short period of eighteen years churches and school-houses, colleges and academies have risen, phœnix-like, out of the ashes of a terrible and devastating war. These institutions crown the hills and dot the valleys throughout the entire South, many of them standing to-day on the very ramparts which, in by-gone days, were thrown up for purposes of destruction. So much has freedom triumphed over slavery, so much peace over war, so much has the world moved. The society, whose anniversary we celebrate to-day, has, of itself alone, established twenty-five of these institutions, supported in the field for the last sixteen years one hundred teachers, and in that time given instruction to seventy-five thousand pupils. The large majority of these pupils become the instructors of others; and so the grand work goes on and on, and shall go until that Southern land is redeemed from the errors of the past, and the manhood of the negro vindicated before the country and the world.

I spoke of the number of the schools. Not less noticeable is their character. The first school-houses for the freedmen were cheaply built of wood for temporary purposes. In these the fort was to be held until, his probation being over, the advancement of the negro should warrant the erection of more costly and substantial buildings. To-day the buildings for the same people are, many of them, models of architectural beauty, and have cost all the way from ten to twenty, to thirty, to forty, to fifty, and, I believe, that Jubilee Hall, at Fisk University, reached the enormous sum of one hundred thousand dollars; and still they are building, building in Georgia and building in Mississippi, building in Arkansas and building in Louisiana, building and educating through the Christian benevolence of the Slaters and the Stones and the Gammons.

Now, what do these buildings mean, these costly buildings of brick and stone, built upon broad and deep and solid foundations? Some few years ago, when we were about to build Chrisman Hall, at Clark University, we found upon the grounds some stone which it was thought might be used for foundation purposes. On some question arising, however, as to its durability, a small piece was taken to the city and tested. The information received with regard to it was, that that stone would crumble, perhaps, but certainly not under a thousand years; and so, friends, we ventured to rest upon foundations hewn out of that stone, the beautiful edifice now known as Chrisman Hall. But, I ask again, what do these thousand years' foundations mean? Mean? Ah, verily, they mean much. They mean permanence. They mean that the capability of the Negro to acquire knowledge is no longer a doubtful problem in the minds of those who know him best, but a fact, and a serious fact, which, for the good of the nation and all concerned, must be attended to, and the sooner the better.

Another fact which bears significance is the character of the work done in these schools. These schools are Christian schools. In them the Bible is supreme, and all the instruction given is more or less seasoned with its teachings. In these schools labor is taught to be honorable, and idleness to be dishonorable, In these schools is taught loyalty to one's God, to one's country, and to one's convictions. The teachers who fill their chairs are required to be persons not only of good moral character, but also of good Christian character, so that no opportunity is given to infidelity or loose religion to creep in and desecrate those halls which, with so much money and so much labor and so much blood have been consecrated to God and humanity.

It is impossible for any thoughtful person to travel through the South to-day, and not feel that in the midst of much that is uncomely and disjointed there is, nevertheless, springing up a new civilization, a civilization that may yet reflect new light upon other sections of the country. There are, as you doubtless know, those who do not approve of the old methods of education, those who claim, and with some reason, perhaps, that the older institutions do not develop the man fully; that they do not fit young men for lives of independence, for lives of active, busy usefulness; that they pay too much attention to the ornamental, and too little to the useful, the practical. Whether this is so or not, there seems to be at present a fair prospect of inaugurating a different order of things in these newly founded schools of the South, a prospect of developing or expanding, if you please, Mr. Parton's idea of the American university of the future, a place where the hand shall be trained along with the head, a place from which, when a young man is graduated, he will not feel compelled to teach or to preach or to be an editor, when he might serve God and his country better by being a machinist or a wood worker. The tendency in the schools of the freedmen is towards the establishment of industrial departments in connection with them. Some have already established them, and more are doing so.

At Clark University we have now a school of carpentry, in which young men are taught not only how to use tools, but also how to draw plans and make specifications. Lectures in architecture are also given. We have, too, a blacksmith shop, where the boys are taught to heat and pound and shape the iron, that grand old metal, by whose use is measured the progress of man's civilization. Still more, we have a model home, a school of domestic economy, the crown and capstone of all the rest, the place in which our girls are to be taught how to sew and how to knit, how to cut and how to make, how to cook and how to— well, in short, ladies, if you will have it—become worthy wives of worthy men, presiding with sweet and queenly dignity over the affairs of well-regulated Christian homes.

The wisdom and foresight exercised in the establishment of these industrial departments are apparent. We can not all be teachers and preachers and lawyers and doctors. This has never been the condition of any people, and the colored people are no exception. Somebody must push the saw and drive the plane. Somebody must plow. There must be somewhere among us a strong, intelligent, virtuous middle class, the salt of society in all ages. Moreover, the demand for skilled labor becomes more and more imperative, and, unless the ranks of the colored mechanics and artisans of the South can be recruited from these schools, or some other schools, if you please, with workmen of a higher intelligence, the South will be flooded with foreigners to meet the demand. This, of course, would be bad for the Negro, but, perhaps, worse for the South and the nation; for, with Europe in her present condition, an influx of foreigners may be accompanied with an influx of dangerous isms—Romanism and Fenianism and Socialism and Communism and Nihilism, and all those isms whose arguments in the settlement of social questions are dynamite and assassination. Surely, then, it is as politic as it is provident in the leaders of our educational work in the South to guard against this train of evils by educating and training for the management of our ever-increasing industries a people born to the soil, a people whose characteristics, tested during two centuries and a half, have been found to be love, affection, gentleness, fidelity, forgiveness, and whose only crime has been the color of their skin. This, then, in brief, is what the Christian Church has done and is doing for us.

Have the colored people improved under this Christian guidance and direction? This, I think, will be apparent to all except those whose prejudices blind their eyes to facts. The

Negro at the close of the war, like his blessed Master, had not where to lay his head. To-day, in the State of Georgia alone, according to the very latest report of the comptroller-general, this same Negro has accumulated property valued at the handsome sum of $6,589,876. According to the same report his increase of property for the last year has been $111,825. This certainly shows, to some extent at least, that he is industrious, economical, and provident. Indeed, when we consider in the face of what opposition this accumulation has been made, and when we consider also the unreasonably low wages for which he has been compelled to work—wages for farm laborers ranging the greater part of the time from forty to fifty cents a day, inclusive of board—I say, when we take these things into consideration, his material prosperity seems little less than astounding.

Need I pause here to convince you of his intellectual improvement? Is not this axiomatic? Need I tell you that in eighteen years we have reared up among us sixteen thousand school-teachers? that these teachers are to-day conducting nearly all the schools for colored youth throughout the entire South? These teachers, as a whole, may not be as thoroughly furnished and equipped for their work as the teachers of the Boston grammar-schools. It would be strange if they were. Nevertheless, I feel free to say that the average colored teacher of the South to-day will compare very favorably with the white teacher of considerably less than a century ago.

The late Dr. Sears, in the Summer of 1880, in an address delivered at Saratoga before the teachers of the country, on "Educational Progress in the United States during the Last Fifty Years," brought to light some significant facts. After showing clearly the sad condition of the schools of New England, and the wretched incompetency of the teachers of that day, he turns southward, and quotes from a book published in Wilmington, Delaware, in 1791, in which Mr. Robert Coram deplores the condition of the schools in that section of country, in the following language: "The country schools," he says, "are in every respect despicable, wretched, and contemptible. The teachers are generally foreigners, shamefully deficient in every qualification, and not seldom addicted to gross vices. One calls the first letter of the alphabet *awe*, and the children are beaten and cuffed to forget their former teaching. When the next schoolmaster is introduced he calls the first letter ă, as in mat, and the school undergoes another reform. At his removal a third is introduced, who calls the first letter hay."

It may be well, too, for you to know that many of the young men, completing higher courses in the schools of the freedmen, are finding their way to your older institutions here in the North for the purpose of studying the professions, and the professors of those institutions give most flattering reports of their scholarship. I am acquainted with some of these young men. I am, certainly, familiarly acquainted with three who, being graduated from Atlanta University, found their way to Massachusetts, where one passed with pretty good grace through a theological course at the historic seminary at Andover, another through a similar course at Newton, and the third is now finishing his course of law in Boston University.

Need I inform you that within eighteen years there has been created among us a reading public that demands to-day two hundred and thirty newspapers, edited and managed by colored men? And all this, too, while some long-visaged persons have been stroking their beards and whining over the Negro problem. I tell you, friends, the most important factor in this so-called Negro problem is the negro himself. The doomed man on the way to the gallows said to the crowd thronging and hurrying to see the execution: "Don't hurry so, friends; there will be no fun until I get there." He who, in the light of to-day, leaves the Negro out of the Negro problem, leaves Hamlet out of Hamlet. Give the Negro a fair chance, and he will work out his own salvation. Hitherto he has literally had to do this with fear and trembling.

I wish to refer to one more fact in connection with the intellectual improvement of the Negro. Some few years ago, when the yellow fever, with its pestilential scourge, was smiting so fearfully certain sections of the South, many of the students of the Meharry Medical College, connected with the Central Tennessee College, went forth into those fields of danger and of death, and labored so faithfully and so successfully among *whites* as well as blacks, as to win for themselves public notice, public praise, and public gratitude. Yes, friends, when the lip is quivering and the eye is fading, when the whole head is sick and the whole heart is faint, men will not hesitate to receive medical assistance even from a black hand.

But it becomes me now, I suppose, to speak of the moral condition of my people. To estimate fairly their improvement in this direction, it would be necessary to realize, if possible, the depth of degradation to which two hundred and fifty years of thralldom had sunk them, and to take into consideration, at the same time, the fact that the moral nature of man everywhere and among every people is by far the most difficult to train. This being so, what must be the task to repair it, after it has been bruised and maimed and twisted and gnarled and distorted? A crooked limb, by proper appliances, may be straightened. A bone of the body may be broken and set, and become even stronger in the fractured part; but man can not sin and be strong. The violation of the moral law means, in every instance, the sapping of moral foundations, the weakening of the moral nature. When, therefore, I consider by what processes, during two centuries, the moral groundwork of my people was undermined and shaken, it is to me no wonder that many of them are to-day found immoral. The greater wonder is that their moral perception has not been entirely swept away. Many people, however, and those especially who stigmatize us as a race peculiarly immoral, do not reason in this way. They do not seem to recognize that slavery was a school ill adapted to the producing of pure and upright characters. Can you rob a man continually of his honest earnings and not teach him to steal? Can you ignore the sanctity of marriage and the family relation and not inculcate lewdness? Can you constantly govern a man with the lash and expect him always to speak truth? If you can do these things, then, verily are my people peculiarly dishonest, impure, and untruthful. But our enemies demand of us perfection. They are unreasonable. They require among us, in twenty short years, a state of moral rectitude which they themselves, with far more favorable opportunities, have not reached in one hundred times twenty. They are unphilosophical, for they do not perceive that diseases are more quickly contracted than cured. *Natura infirmitatis humanæ tardiora sunt remedia quam mala.*

Very amusing, too, it is to listen to the hue and cry sent up every little while against Negro immoralities; such a cry and a howl as went up but recently from the swamps of Mississippi, and are still reverberating through the country with jarring sound.

Very amusing, I say, it is to listen to these cries against Negro immoralities, when the same immoralities are continually cropping out among the white people, professedly our superiors. How many times within the last two decades has this nation had to hang its head in shame because of the dishonesty of its public men! What about Credit Mobilier and the Tammany frauds? What about whisky rings? What about cipher dispatches? What about Star Route trials? What about the stuffing of ballot-boxes? What about the defalcation and impeachment of high State officials? And so on and so on *ad infinitum?*

But, sir, I am not here to apologize for the vices and immoralities of my people. That such things do exist I do know and I do deplore. Neither, sir, am I here to checkmate what they have done with what somebody else has done. But I am here, sir, to fling back the charge so frequently made against them as a people peculiarly immoral and lewd. We have not had a fair chance in this country; but in proportion to our opportunities we can show as many good, virtuous, law-abiding citizens as any other race on this continent. Wherever in the South Christian education has reached the freedmen it has awakened in them a taste for the true and the beautiful. This may be seen in the changed manner of living of many of them. The dirty shanty and clumsy log-cabin in which, in former times, so many were accustomed to be huddled together, are retreating, step by step, before the steady advance of neat and cosy cottages. Christian homes, the strength of any nation, are being built up, decorated with the beauties and improvements of modern art.

I am proud, too, to know that in this transition period of ours we have had among us a few public men of unimpeachable character. When Oscar Dunn was lieutenant-governor of Louisiana a certain white man, interested in a bill before the Legislature, endeavored, by the use of money, to secure Mr. Dunn's influence in favor of that bill. The reply of that noble Negro was as withering as it is laconic: "Sir," said he, "my conscience is not for sale." In that memorable presidential election, when Messrs. Hayes and Tilden were candidates, a colored man in one of those Southern States, at that time a member of the electoral college, was approached by a white man, and offered fifty thousand dollars for his vote for Mr. Tilden, being informed, at the same time, that it was a "graveyard secret," and that, if he ever exposed the offerer of that sum death would be the penalty. I am proud to say that that brave and faithful man rejected with scorn the proffered bribe. Would Anglo-Saxon morality have stood a better test against gilded corruption?

Let us, friends, learn lessons from these things. Let us rise above low, narrow, absurd, wicked discriminations against men on account of their race, their color, or their nationality. Let us endeavor to repair the wrongs of the past. Let us be just and let us be humane. Let us see to it that in the future fair play is given to that six and a half millions of people in your midst who have felled your forests, tilled your fields, developed the resources of a section of your country, received insult and injury untold and unspeakable, yet, in the midst of it all, have beautifully illustrated,

"How sublime a thing it is
To suffer and be strong."

Let us, I say, be wise. Let us draw nearer to each other, that we may understand each other the better; and as the various colors in the solar spectrum are blended in giving one brilliant and glorious light, so even, in the bright future now dawning upon this nation, let all our efforts and all our energies be blended in promoting harmony and good will, and in hastening on the happy time when this country shall be in the spirit, as well as in the letter, what God evidently intended it should be, the asylum for the oppressed of all lands, the home of the free, the country in which, untrammeled by priest or by potentate, beneath his own vine and fig tree, with naught to molest or make him afraid, every man, of every race, may enjoy the blessings of Almighty God.

OUR OBLIGATION TO THE FREEDMEN.

BY REV. J. N. FITZGERALD, D D.,

RECORDING SECRETARY OF THE MISSIONARY SOCIETY.

THOUSANDS of years ago the question was asked, "What can the man do that cometh after the king?" Varying slightly from this, I am constrained to-day to ask, What can the man do that cometh after *all* the kings? From ten o'clock in the morning until ten o'clock at night, during the four days just past, able and eloquent men have discoursed from this platform upon the subject of educating the illiterate people of these United States. More than fifty addresses have been delivered, covering every point and presenting the topic in every light. And yet I am asked at this time to speak concerning the Freedmen's Aid Society, and our obligation to see that its educational work is performed.

I. It has been often said that man is the only creature capable of education. Animals remain the same so far as instinct and perception are concerned; but man, as the door opens before him, constantly enlarges the sphere of his activity, and advances toward higher planes of both thought and action. Circumstances may conspire to degrade him and hold him near the level of the brute; but, on the other hand, influences may combine to lead him up to a position beside the most exalted, where he may successfully resist, and indeed control, most of the forces of nature, animate and inanimate. Under such *favorable* influences we seek to place the freedman—hence our cry is, *Education*. This cry is being sounded from hilltop to hilltop of this broad land, and it shall not die away until those in whose interest it has been raised shall have been lifted to the place which God designs they shall occupy. But what is education? It is the expansion, enlargement, growth of the mental faculties. It is not so much putting in new things as bringing out the things that are in already. It is the "full and harmonious development of all the powers and capacities of the man."

Development has been God's order during all the ages, and it is the watchword of civilization and Christianity to-day. As art and science advance they are everywhere hailed with delight, and men and nations contribute of their substance to speed these twin sisters on their way. Visit the highly cultivated and richly adorned grounds which, at so many points, have superseded the wilderness and the desert, and compute the amount that has been and is being expended for the development of flowers, fruit, and grain. Consider the horse, the cow, the sheep, the dog, for whose *physical* improvement millions are spent every year; and then compare with those millions the small sum that is doled out annually for the *mental* improvement of those members of the human family who, within the bounds of our own land and under the shadow of our own Church have been held so long in the chains of ignorance. More remarkable still does this seem in view of the fact that mental qualities, and moral, too, are quite as transmissible as physical qualities are. In building up and strengthening the mental powers of a man we accomplish a work of vast importance for his progeny. This fact ought to be a wonderful inspiration to us to aid the multitudes whose intellectual faculties are only waiting for the application of that force which shall draw forth their powers and make them a mighty influence for good.

Men who have been steadily recognized as the enemies of the black race meet us with the declaration that no appliance, no effort, no skill can evolve from the members of that race any thing of strength; that there is in them no force capable of development. It would be quite as reasonable to declare that the water which has never felt the influence of strong heat is capable of no change that will give it power, or that the seed, which has been always kept from contact with the earth, possesses no vitality. To those who have neither knowledge nor faith in regard to such matters, it may seem that there is no force, either manifest or hidden, in the water or the seed; but to the man who either believes or knows, the result seems easily attainable, and he will confidently apply to the water the heat that will produce the irresistible steam, and with equal confidence he will sow the seed in the earth and wait for the rain and the sunshine to draw forth from it the tender blade, the stalk, and the full corn in the ear. With the same assurance the workers in the grand cause which we advocate to-day, bring to bear upon the mind and the heart of the freedmen those influences which they *know* will develop intellectual and moral force, and make man more like God. Thus they accomplish the grandest of missions. Others may demonstrate the powers of heat and cold, of air and fire and water, of light and electricity—indeed of all the elements of matter, either separate or combined—but *they* will show forth the powers that so long have lain dormant in the minds of our country's illiterate freedmen; and as those powers become more fully aroused, thus enabling their possessors to withstand and overthrow error, and to comprehend and elaborate truth, the world will applaud and God will approve.

It is well to endow with large sums institutions which will afford to those who have already achieved some success in the educational field, the opportunity to advance toward the mastery; but it is *not* well to do this at the risk of doing nothing for those who have not yet had the first opportunity to learn the A, B, C of their native tongue. If there be not sufficient funds for both classes, let us spend for those who have *no* education, rather than for those who have enjoyed great advantages, and are now seeking higher attainments. Let us not neglect the patient whose life still hangs in the balance, for the purpose of nursing the one who is already convalescent and able to minister to his own need. The illiterate should be well started in the path of education, and then, as has been often demonstrated, he will put forth effort in his own behalf that will be productive of large results. Now he can do nothing for himself. In case he secures an hour of leisure he is at a loss to know how to spend it. He can not take a book or paper, and pass that hour in reading; hence he must seek other means of employment or enjoyment, and in the search he is often led into company where the most evil of lessons are to be learned and the most evil of habits formed. It is no answer to say, that after being sufficiently taught he may read that which will demoralize and debauch, for where there is one vile volume there are many good ones; and where one man is harmed many are helped by reading that which is nearest at hand.

This development of the freedman is necessary that he may the better apprehend and comprehend his rights and duties, and that the generations which are to follow him may start at a higher point. He has claims which have been long ignored, and which should be now asserted and enforced. He has obligations to discharge which will be more perfectly met when he comes to a fuller understanding of them. He is to be succeeded by others who, if they can but commence the race of life under improved conditions, will run the more successfully and the more surely gain the prize.

The prime object of the society the anniversary of whose organization we celebrate to-day, was to accomplish these things for the freedmen, but the needs of other classes have become so apparent that now the society extends a helping hand to the illiterate whites also; and yet the order still is, that the prime object shall be first attained—after that, the other. The reason for this distinction is found in the fact that the black man was prohibited from accepting relief even when it was tendered, and was obliged to remain in his low condition, regardless of the intensity of his desire to rise. He is, therefore, an *enforced* illiterate, and for this reason we seek to educate *him first*. The very name by which he is designated awakens deepest interest. A *freeman* may, and under the old law must, have been free from the moment of his birth, but a *freedman* must once have been a slave.

How full of meaning, then, is that single letter "d!" Standing directly upon the line of emancipation, it tells the story of DELIVERANCE, and speaks of the dawning of a better day.

Backward from the line it points to DARKNESS, DEGRADATION, and DESPAIR. It tells of the lash, the hound, and the block; of prostitution, illegitimacy, and brutality—indeed, of all the horrors of a system which, for viciousness, is without a parallel.

Forward from the line it points to DAYLIGHT, DEVELOPMENT, and DIGNITY. Its announcement is, that the golden dawning which we have been permitted to behold will be followed by a light that shall shine more and more unto the perfect day. It declares not only that the shackles are broken, and the lash laid aside, and the hound enchained, and the block consumed, so that the prostrated and bleeding *body* can arise, but that forces are at work to emancipate the *mind*, and infuse into it energy and strength that will enable it to reach out toward *another* freedom, with which the freedom of the body is not for a moment to be compared.

The backward pointing of this significant character is toward the DEVILISH. Its forward pointing is toward the DIVINE. It rises to our view as both historian and prophet, telling us what was, and what is yet to be. By its history we are saddened, and led to pray that such history may never be repeated. By its prophecy we are gladdened, and inspired with a faith that enables us, even now, to witness the complete fulfillment of that which is foretold.

II. Let us now scan the grounds of our obligation to aid this society in the education of the freedmen.

1. The general ground of obligation *to minister to those who are in need.* In support of this it is necessary only to refer to the words of Christ as recorded in the twenty-fifth chapter of Matthew, commencing at the thirty-first verse.

2. The ground of *compensation.*

This nation is the black man's debtor. The charges are written in blood on every battlefield, aye, on every cotton-field, in this fair land. Over against these charges some credits have been placed, but they are so few and for such small amounts that the balance still remaining seems well-nigh fabulous.

The Methodist Episcopal Church also is largely indebted to the colored race. John Stewart, the John Baptist of our Missionary Society, laid upon us a debt that is beyond computation. In obedience to the command which came directly to him from God he journeyed through a wilderness and prepared a glorious way. As we look upon him and Jonathan Pointer, a man of his own color, who speedily joined hands with him in the work, we can not resist the conclusion that one of the greatest developments of our Church was brought about through them. They started the work of Home Missions, which has since been carried on so vigorously by us, and been so greatly blessed to the good of thousands of the white as well as of the red people of America.

We remember, too, that God's call to our Church to enter *foreign* fields was made through colored men, and that the work which was commenced in response to that call has been so extended as to reach all lands and all races, and to bring upon them the abundant blessings of the Gospel of Christ. And now, that the hour to supply the black man's need has arrived, shall we hesitate to pay that which we have withheld so long? The term of his service was so protracted, and the harvest resulting from his labors is so great, that it will be impossible for us to pay him adequately. Nevertheless such compensation as we have the power to make should be made, and that right early.

3. We owe it as *restitution.*

Illiteracy is upon the freedman because of our wrongful course toward him; hence what we do to dispel that illiteracy is less than charity, and less than compensation. It is *restitution*. *And restitution is the first duty of man*. Some persons declare that the condition of the slave in America was far better than his previous condition in Africa; that we have brought him from barbarism, and thus accomplished much for him. But, we answer, Bad as are the barbarism and all the other evils of "the dark continent," they are neither worse nor more ruinous than that system which the founder of our Church characterized as "the sum of all villainies." The bondman may have been brought to the "Sunny South," but, at the same time, he was placed in the midst of the death damps of slavery. He may have stood upon the ground where many a battle was fought and won for freedom, but he had the sorrowful consciousness that he was a slave. So long as the fetters remained upon him it was vain to tell of his charming surroundings. The response to the entire recital would be given in Dryden's beautiful words:

"O give me liberty!
For were even paradise my prison,
Still I should long to leap the crystal walls."

Death is to be preferred to slavery. Therefore we say that the wrong done by us in making and keeping the black man a slave, and in forcing ignorance upon him, thus robbing him of a priceless heritage, calls for atonement—for *restitution*.

We must, however, bear in mind that those who were emancipated, and are now near us, were by birth Americans, not Africans, and that after being born beneath the stars and stripes they were denied the rights which the flag promised. Not only did we refuse to lift them, but, by our statutory enactments we laid weights upon them to keep them down. Yet, in the face of all this, there are many among us who ignobly and heartlessly refuse to make any return. Others acknowledge the obligation and meet it in small degree, but for so doing they claim great credit. They boastfully point to the million and a quarter of dollars which this society has expended for the elevation of the freedman, and claim that the contributors toward that sum should receive large commendation. As well might the brethren of Joseph have claimed credit for taking him out of the pit. As well might Darius have claimed credit for commanding that they should take Daniel up out of the den of lions; or Nebuchadnezzar for calling the Hebrew children forth from the fiery furnace. The aid we give the freedman is not that which the good Samaritan afforded. It is rather that which one extends to the drowning man whom he wickedly threw into the sea. Surprisingly strange is this request for commendation. Credit for nursing the one whom we have unjustly beaten, and into whose blood we have infused the deadly poison! Credit for bearing a loaf of bread to him whose harvests we have appropriated to our own use for centuries! Credit for righting, in slight measure, a wrong committed by ourselves, and which is so gigantic that time itself can not afford sufficient years in which to completely repair it! When justice shall destroy her scales, when the broken law of God shall require no satisfaction, when sin shall need no atonement, then let the citizen of this Republic who seeks credit for service rendered the freedman come forth and present his claim.

Until then let no colored man come asking these educational supplies as *charity*, but let him come pointing to the past and claiming his due. Let him say to the white people throughout this land, You stopped my ears, you put the scales upon my eyes, you dwarfed my intellect, you stunted all my best faculties, and now I come, not begging for charity, but demanding recompense—*restitution*. I come claiming *mine own*, that with it I may commence the ascent of the mountain, far up the sides, and possibly upon the summit, of which I might have stood long years ago had it not been for the unchristian, unbrotherly, unmanly, and wicked influences which you have exerted against me. I come echoing the words of the divine One: "Render, therefore, unto Cæsar the things which are Cæsar's, and unto God the things that are God's."

THE BLACK WOMAN OF THE SOUTH:

Her Neglects and Her Needs.

BY REV. ALEXANDER CRUMMELL, D. D.,

RECTOR OF ST. LUKE'S CHURCH, WASHINGTON, D. C.

IT is an age clamorous everywhere for the dignities, the grand prerogatives, and the glory of woman. There is not a country in Europe where she has not risen somewhat above the degradation of centuries, and pleaded successfully for a new position and a higher vocation. As the result of this new reformation we see her, in our day, seated in the lecture-rooms of ancient universities, rivaling her brothers in the fields of literature, the grand creators of ethereal art, the participants in noble civil franchises, the moving spirit in grand reformations, and the guide, agent, or assistant in all the noblest movements for the civilization and regeneration of man.

In these several lines of progress the American woman has run on in advance of her sisters in every other quarter of the globe. The advantage she has received, the rights and prerogatives she has secured for herself, are unequaled by any other class of women in the world. It will not be thought amiss, then, that I come here to-day to present to your consideration the one grand exception to this general superiority of women, viz., "THE BLACK WOMAN OF THE SOUTH."

In speaking to-day of the "black woman," I must needs make a very clear distinction. The African race in this country is divided into two classes, that is—the *colored people* and the *negro population*. In the census returns of 1860 this whole population was set down at 4,500,000. Of these, the *colored* numbered 500,000; the *black* or *negro* population at 4,000,000. But notice these other broad lines of demarkation between them. The colored people, while indeed but *one-fifth* of the number of the blacks, counted more men and women who could read and write than the whole 4,000,000 of their brethren in bondage. A like disparity showed itself in regard to their *material* condition. The 500,000 colored people were absolutely richer in lands and houses than the many millions of their degraded kinsmen.

The causes of these differences are easily discovered. The colored population received, in numerous cases, the kindness and generosity of their white kindred—white fathers and relatives. Forbidden by law to marry the negro woman, very many slaveholders took her as the wife despite the law; and when children were begotten every possible recognition was given those children, and they were often cared for, educated, and made possessors of property. Sometimes they were sent to Northern schools, sometimes to France or England. Not unfrequently whole families, nay, at times, whole colonies, were settled in Western or Northern towns, and largely endowed with property. The colored population, moreover, was, as compared with the negro, the *urban* population. They were brought in large numbers to the cities, and thus largely partook of the civilization and refinement of the whites. They were generally the domestic servants of their masters, and thus, brought in contact with their superiors, they gained a sort of education which never came to the field hands, living in rude huts on the plantations. All this, however casual it may seem, was a merciful providence, by which some gleams of light and knowledge came, indirectly, to the race in this land.

The rural or plantation population of the South was made up almost entirely of people of pure negro blood. And this brings out also the other disastrous fact, namely, that this large black population has been living from the time of their introduction into America, a period of more than two hundred years, in a state of unlettered rudeness. The Negro all this time has been an intellectual starveling. This has been more especially the condition of the black woman of the South. Now and then a black man has risen above the debased condition of his people. Various causes would contribute to the advantage of the *men*: the relation of servants to superior masters; attendance at courts with them; their presence at political meetings; listening to table-talk behind their chairs; traveling as valets; the privilege of books and reading in great houses, and with indulgent masters—all these served to lift up a black *man* here and there to something like superiority. But no such fortune fell to the lot of the plantation woman. The black woman of the South was left perpetually in a state of hereditary darkness and rudeness. Since the day of Phillis Wheatly no Negress in this land (that is, in the South) has been raised above the level of her sex. The lot of the black *man* on the plantation has been sad and desolate enough; but the fate of the black woman has been awful! Her entire existence from the day when she first landed, a naked victim of the slave-trade, has been degradation in its extremest forms.

In her girlhood all the delicate tenderness of her sex has been rudely outraged. In the field, in the rude cabin, in the press-room, in the factory, she was thrown into the companionship of coarse and ignorant men. No chance was given her for delicate reserve or tender modesty. From her childhood she was the doomed victim of the grossest passions. All the virtues of her sex were utterly ignored. If the instinct of chastity asserted itself, then she had to fight like a tigress for the ownership and possession of her own person; and, ofttimes, had to suffer pains and lacerations for her virtuous self-assertion. When she reached maturity all the tender instincts of her womanhood were ruthlessly violated. At the age of marriage—always prematurely anticipated under slavery—she was mated, as the stock of the plantation were mated, *not* to be the companion of a loved and chosen husband, but to be the breeder of human cattle, for the field or the auction-block. With that mate she went out, morning after morning to toil, as a common field hand. As it was *his*, so likewise was it her lot to wield the heavy hoe, or to follow the plow, or to gather in the crops. She was a "hewer of wood and a drawer of water." She was a common field-hand. She had to keep her place in the gang from morn till eve, under the burden of a heavy task, or under the stimulus or the fear of a cruel lash. She was a picker of cotton. She labored at the sugar mill and in the tobacco factory. When, through weariness or sickness, she has fallen behind her allotted task then came, as punishment, the fearful stripes upon her shrinking, lacerated flesh.

Her home life was of the most degrading nature. She lived in the rudest huts, and partook of the coarsest food, and dressed in the scantiest garb, and slept, in multitudinous cabins, upon the hardest boards!

Thus she continued a beast of burden down to the period of those maternal anxieties which, in ordinary civilized life, give repose, quiet, and care to expectant mothers. But, under the slave system, few such relaxations were allowed. And so it came to pass that little children were ushered into this world under conditions which many cattle raisers would not suffer for their flocks or herds. Thus she became the mother of children. But even then there was for her no suretyship of motherhood, or training, or control. Her own offspring were *not* her own. She and husband and children were all the property of others. All these sacred ties were constantly snapped and cruelly sundered. *This* year she had one husband; and next year, through some auction sale, she might be separated from him and mated with another. There was no sanctity of family, no binding tie of marriage, none of the fine felicities and the endearing affections of home. None of these things were the lot of Southern black women. Instead thereof a gross barbarism which tended to blunt the tender sensibilities, to obliterate feminine delicacy and womanly shame, came down as her heritage from generation to generation; and it seems a miracle of providence and grace that, notwithstanding these terrible circumstances, so much struggling virtue lingered amid these rude cabins, that so much womanly worth and sweetness abided in their bosoms, as slaveholders themselves have borne witness to.

But some of you will ask: "Why bring up these sad memories of the past? Why distress us with these dead and departed cruelties?" Alas, my friends, these are not dead things. Remember that

"The evil that men do lives after them."

The evil of gross and monstrous abominations, the evil of great organic institutions crop out long after the departure of the institutions themselves. If you go to Europe you will find not only the roots, but likewise many of the deadly fruits of the old Feudal system still surviving in several of its old states and kingdoms. So, too, with slavery. The eighteen years of freedom have not obliterated all its deadly marks from either the souls or bodies of the black woman. The conditions of life, indeed, have been modified since emancipation; but it still maintains that the black woman is the Pariah woman of this land! We have, indeed, degraded women, immigrants from foreign lands. In their own countries some of them were so low in the social scale that they were yoked with the cattle to plow the fields. They were rude, unlettered, coarse, and benighted. But when they reach *this* land there comes an end to their degraded condition.

"They touch our country and their shackles fall."

As soon as they become grafted into the stock of American life they partake at once of all its large gifts and its noble resources.

Not so with the black woman of the South. Freed, legally, she has been; but the act of emancipation had no talismanic influence to reach to and alter and transform her degrading social life.

When that proclamation was issued she might have heard the whispered words in her every hut, "Open Sesame;" but, so far as her humble domicile and her degraded person was concerned, there was no invisible but gracious Genii who, on the instant, could transmute the rudeness of her hut into instant elegance, and change the crude surroundings of her home into neatness, taste, and beauty.

The truth is, "Emancipation Day" found her a prostrate and degraded being; and, although it has brought numerous advantages to her sons, it has produced but the simplest changes in her social and domestic condition. She is still the crude, rude, ignorant mother. Remote from cities, the dweller still in the old plantation hut, neighboring to the sulky, disaffected master class, who still think her freedom was a personal robbery of themselves, none of the "fair humanities" have visited her humble home. The light of knowledge has not fallen upon her eyes. The fine domesticities which give the charm to family life, and which, by the refinement and delicacy of womanhood, preserve the civilization of nations, have not come to *her*. She has still the rude, coarse labor of men. With her rude husband she still shares the hard service of a field-hand. Her house, which shelters, perhaps, some six or eight children, embraces but two rooms. Her furniture is of the rudest kind. The clothing of the household is scant and of the coarsest material, has ofttimes the garniture of rags; and for herself and offspring is marked, not seldom, by the absence of both hats and shoes. She has never been taught to sew, and the field labor of slavery times has kept her ignorant of the habitudes of neatness and the requirements of order. Indeed, coarse food, coarse clothes, coarse living, coarse manners, coarse companions, coarse surroundings, coarse neighbors, both white and black, yea, every thing coarse, down to the coarse, ignorant, senseless religion, which excites her sensibilities and starts her passions, go to make up the life of the masses of black women in the hamlets and villages of the rural South.

This is the state of black womanhood. Take the girlhood of this same region, and it presents the same aspect, save that in large districts the white man has not forgotten the olden times of slavery, and, with, indeed, the deepest sentimental abhorrence of "amalgamation," still thinks that the black girl is to be perpetually the victim of his lust! In the larger towns and in cities our girls, in common schools and academies, are receiving superior culture. Of the fifteen thousand colored school teachers in the South, more than half are colored young women, educated since emancipation. But even these girls, as well as their more ignorant sisters in rude huts, are followed and tempted and insulted by the ruffianly element of Southern society, who think that black *men* have no rights which white men should regard, and black *women* no virtue which white men should respect!

And now look at the *vastness* of this degradation. If I had been speaking of the population of a city, or a town, or even a village, the tale would be a sad and melancholy one. But I have brought before you the condition of millions of women. According to the census of 1880 there were, in the Southern States, 3,327,678 females of all ages of the African race. Of these there were 674,365 girls between twelve and twenty, 1,522,696 between twenty and eighty. "These figures," remarks an observant friend of mine, "are startling!" And when you think that the masses of these women live in the rural districts; that they grow up in rudeness and ignorance; that their former masters are using few means to break up their hereditary degradation, you can easily take in the pitiful condition of this population, and forecast the inevitable future to multitudes of females, unless a mighty special effort is made for the improvement of the black womanhood of the South.

I know the practical nature of the American mind, I know how the question of values intrudes itself into even the domain of philanthropy; and, hence, I shall not be astonished if the query suggests itself, whether special interest in the black woman will bring any special advantage to the American nation.

Let me dwell for a few moments upon this phase of the subject. Possibly the view I am about suggesting has never before been presented to the American mind. But, Negro as I am,

I shall make no apology for venturing the claim that the Negress is one of the most interesting of all the classes of women on the globe. I am speaking of her, not as a perverted and degraded creature, but in her natural state, with her native instincts and peculiarities.

Let me repeat just here the words of a wise, observing, tenderhearted philanthropist, whose name and worth and words have attained celebrity. It is fully forty years ago since the celebrated Dr. Channing said: "We are holding in bondage one of the best races of the human family. The Negro is among the mildest, gentlest of men. He is singularly susceptible of improvement from abroad. . . . His nature is affectionate, easily touched, and hence he is more open to religious improvement than the white man. . . . The African carries with him much more than we the genius of a meek, long-suffering, loving virtue."*

I should feel ashamed to allow these words to fall from my lips if it were not necessary to the lustration of the character of my black sisters of the South. I do not stand here to-day to plead for the black man. He is a man; and if he is weak he must go to the wall. He is a man; he must fight his own way, and if he is strong in mind and body, he can take care of himself. But for the mothers, sisters, and daughters of my race I have a right to speak. And when I think of their sad condition down South, think, too, that since the day of emancipation hardly any one has lifted up a voice in their behalf, I feel it a duty and a privilege to set forth their praises and to extol their excellencies. For, humble and benighted as she is, the black woman of the South is one of the queens of womanhood. If there is any other woman on this earth who in native aboriginal qualities is her superior, I know not where she is to be found; for, I do say, that in tenderness of feeling, in genuine native modesty, in large disinterestedness, in sweetness of disposition and deep humility, in unselfish devotedness, and in warm, motherly assiduities, the Negro woman is unsurpassed by any other woman on this earth.

The testimony to this effect is almost universal—our enemies themselves being witnesses. You know how widely and how continuously, for generations, the Negro has been traduced, ridiculed, derided. Some of you may remember the journals and

---

*"Emancipation." By Rev. W. E. Channing, D. D. Works of W. E. Channing, D. D. A. U. A. Ed. Pp. 820.

the hostile criticisms of Coleridge and Trollope and Burton, West Indian and African travelers. Very many of you may remember the philosophical disquisitions of the ethnological school of 1847, the contemptuous dissertations of Hunt and Gliddon. But it is worthy of notice in all these cases that the sneer, the contempt, the bitter gibe, have been invariably leveled against the black *man*—never against the black woman! On the contrary, *she* has almost everywhere been extolled and eulogized. The black man was called a stupid, thick-lipped, flat-nosed, long-heeled, empty-headed animal; the link between the baboon and the human being, only fit to be a slave! But everywhere, even in the domains of slavery, how tenderly has the Negress been spoken of! She has been the nurse of childhood. To her all the cares and heart-griefs of youth have been intrusted. Thousands and tens of thousands in the West Indies and in our Southern States have risen up and told the tale of her tenderness, of her gentleness, patience, and affection. No other woman in the world has ever had such tributes to a high moral nature, sweet, gentle love, and unchanged devotedness. And by the memory of my own mother and dearest sisters I can declare it to be true!

Hear the tribute of Michelet: "The Negress, of all others, is the most loving, the most generating; and this, not only because of her youthful blood, but we must also admit, for the richness of her heart. She is loving among the loving, good among the good (ask the travelers whom she has so often saved). Goodness is creative, it is fruitfulness, it is the very benediction of a holy act. The fact that woman is so fruitful I attribute to her treasures of tenderness, to that ocean of goodness which permeates her heart. . . . Africa is a woman. Her races are feminine. . . . In many of the black tribes of Central Africa the women rule, and they are as intelligent as they are amiable and kind."*

The reference in Michelet to the generosity of the African woman to travelers brings to mind the incident in Mungo Park's travels, where the African women fed, nourished, and saved him. The men had driven him away. They would not even allow him to feed with the cattle; and so, faint, weary, and despairing, he went to a remote hut and lay down on the earth to die. One

---

* "Woman." From the French of M. J. Michelet, page 132. Rudd & Carleton, New York.

woman, touched with compassion, came to him, brought him food and milk, and at once he revived. Then he tells us of the solace and the assiduities of these gentle creatures for his comfort. I give you his own words: "The rites of hospitality thus performed towards a stranger in distress, my worthy benefactress, pointing to the mat, and telling me that I might sleep there without apprehension, called to the female part of her family which had stood gazing on me all the while in fixed astonishment, to resume the task of spinning cotton, in which they continued to employ themselves a great part of the night. They lightened their labors by songs, one of which was composed extempore, for I was myself the subject of it. It was sung by one of the young women, the rest joining in a sort of chime. The air was sweet and plaintive, and the words, literally translated, were these: 'The winds roared and the rains fell; the poor white man, faint and weary, came and sat under our tree. He has no mother to bring him milk, no wife to grind his corn. Let us pity the white man, no mother has he,'" etc., etc.

Perhaps I may be pardoned the intrusion, just here, of my own personal experience. During a residence of nigh twenty years in West Africa, I saw the beauty and felt the charm of the native female character. I saw the native woman in her *heathen* state, and was delighted to see, in numerous tribes, that extraordinary sweetness, gentleness, docility, modesty, and especially those maternal solicitudes which make every African boy both gallant and defender of his mother.

I saw her in her *civilized* state, in Sierra Leone; saw precisely the same characteristics, but heightened, dignified, refined, and sanctified by the training of the schools, the refinements of civilization, and the graces of Christian sentiment and feeling. Of all the memories of foreign travel there are none more delightful than those of the families and the female friends of Freetown.

A French traveler speaks with great admiration of the black ladies of Hayti. "In the towns," he says, "I met all the charms of civilized life. The graces of the ladies of Port-au-Prince will never be effaced from my recollections."[*]

It was, without doubt, the instant discernment of these fine and tender qualities which prompted the touching Sonnet of

[*] See "Jamaica in 1850." By John Bigelow.

Wordsworth, written in 1802, on the occasion of the cruel exile of Negroes from France by the French Government:

"Driven from the soil of France, a female came
From Calais with us, brilliant in array,
A Negro woman like a lady gay,
Yet downcast as a woman fearing blame;
Meek, destitute, as seemed, of hope or aim
She sat, from notice turning not away,
But on all proffered intercourse did lay
A weight of languid speech—or at the same
Was silent, motionless in eyes and face.
Meanwhile those eyes retained their tropic fire,
Which burning independent of the mind,
Joined with the luster of her rich attire
To mock the outcast—O ye heavens be kind!
And feel thou earth for this afflicted race!"*

But I must remember that I am to speak not only of the neglects of the black woman, but also of her needs. And the consideration of her needs suggests the remedy which should be used for the uplifting of this woman from a state of brutality and degradation.

I have two or three plans to offer which, I feel assured, if faithfully used, will introduce widespread and ameliorating influences amid this large population.

(a) The *first* of these is specially adapted to the adult female population of the South, and is designed for more immediate effect. I ask for the equipment and the mission of "sisterhoods" to the black women of the South. I wish to see large numbers of practical Christian women, women of intelligence and piety; women well trained in domestic economy; women who combine delicate sensibility and refinement with industrial acquaintance—scores of such women to go South; to enter every Southern State; to visit "Uncle Tom's Cabin;" to sit down with "Aunt Chloe" and her daughters; to show and teach them the ways and habits of thrift, economy, neatness, and order; to gather them into "Mothers' Meetings" and sewing schools; and by both lectures and "talks" guide these women and their daughters into the modes and habits of clean and orderly housekeeping.

There is no other way, it seems to me, to bring about this domestic revolution.—We can not postpone this reformation to another generation. Postponement is the reproduction of the

---

* Wordsworth. Sonnets dedicated to Liberty.

same evils in numberless daughters now coming up into life, imitators of the crude and untidy habits of their neglected mothers, and the perpetuation of plantation life to another generation. No, the effort must be made immediately, in *this* generation, with the rude, rough, neglected women of the times.

And it is to be done at their own homes, in their own huts. In this work all theories are useless. This is a practical need, and personal as practical. It is emphatically a personal work. It is to be done by example. The "Sister of Mercy," putting aside all fastidiousness, is to enter the humble and, perchance, repulsive cabin of her black sister, and gaining her confidence, is to lead her out of the crude, disordered, and miserable ways of her plantation life into neatness, cleanliness, thrift, and self-respect. In every community women could be found who would gladly welcome such gracious visitations and instructors, and seize with eagerness their lessons and teachings. Soon their neighbors would seek the visitations which had lifted up friends and kinsfolk from inferiority and wretchedness. And then, erelong, whole communities would crave the benediction of these inspiring sisterhoods, and thousands and tens of thousands would hail the advent of these missionaries in their humble cabins. And then the seed of a new and orderly life planted in a few huts and localities, it would soon spread abroad, through the principle of imitation, and erelong, like the Banyan-tree, the beneficent work would spread far and wide through large populations. Doubtless they would be received, first of all, with surprise, for neither they nor their mothers, for two hundred years, have ever known the solicitudes of the great and cultivated for their domestic comfort. But surprise would soon give way to joy and exultation. Mrs. Fanny Kemble Butler, in her work, "Journal of a Residence on a Georgian Plantation in 1838–39," tells us of the amazement of the wretched slave women on her husband's plantation when she went among them, and tried to improve their quarters and to raise them above squalor; and then of their immediate joy and gratitude.

There is nothing original in the suggestion I make for the "Sisters of Mercy." It is no idealistic and impractical scheme I am proposing, no new-fangled notion that I put before you. The Roman Catholic Church has, for centuries, been employing the agency of women in the propagation of her faith and as dispensers of charity. The Protestants of Germany are noted for the effective labors of holy women, not only in the Fatherland but in some of the most successful missions among the heathen in modern times. The Church of England, in that remarkable revival which has lifted her up as by a tidal wave, from the dead passivity of the last century, to an apostolic zeal and fervor never before known in her history, has shown, as one of her main characteristics, the wonderful power of "Sisterhoods," not only in the conversion of reprobates, but in the reformation of whole districts of abandoned men and women. This agency has been one of the most effective instrumentalities in the hands of that special school of devoted men called "Ritualists." Women of every class in that Church, many of humble birth, and as many more from the ranks of the noble, have left home and friends and the choicest circles of society, and given up their lives to the lowliest service of the poor and miserable. They have gone down into the very slums of her great cities, among thieves and murderers and harlots; amid filth and disease and pestilence; and for Christ's sake served and washed and nursed the most repulsive wretches; and then have willingly laid down and died, either exhausted by their labors or poisoned by infectious disease. Any one who will read the life of "Sister Dora" and of Charles Lowder, will see the glorious illustrations of my suggestion. Why can not this be done for the black women of the South?

(b) My *second* suggestion is as follows, and it reaches over to the future. I am anxious for a permanent and uplifting civilization to be engrafted on the Negro race in this land. And this can only be secured through the womanhood of a race. If you want the civilization of a people to reach the very best elements of their being, and then, having reached them, there to abide, as an indigenous principle, you must imbue the *womanhood* of that people with all its elements and qualities. Any movement which passes by the female sex is an ephemeral thing. Without them, no true nationality, patriotism, religion, cultivation, family life, or true social status is a possibility. In *this* matter it takes *two* to make one—mankind is a duality. The *male* may bring, as an exotic, a foreign graft, say of a civilization, to a new people. But what then? Can a graft live or thrive of itself? By no manner of means. It must get vitality from the *stock* into which it is put; and it is the women who give the sap to every human organization which thrives and flourishes on earth.

I plead, therefore, for the establishment of at least one large "INDUSTRIAL SCHOOL" in every Southern State for the black girls of the South. I ask for the establishment of schools which may serve especially the *home* life of the rising womanhood of my race. I am not soliciting for these girls scholastic institutions, seminaries for the cultivation of elegance, conservatories of music, and schools of classical and artistic training. I want such schools and seminaries for the women of my race as much as any other race; and I am glad that there are such schools and colleges, and that scores of colored women are students within their walls.

But this higher style of culture is not what I am aiming after for *this* great need. I am seeking something humbler, more homelike and practical, in which the education of the hand and the use of the body shall be the specialties, and where the intellectual training will be the incident.

Let me state just here definitely what I want for the black girls of the South:

1. I want boarding-schools for the *industrial training* of one hundred and fifty or two hundred of the poorest girls, of the ages of twelve to eighteen years.

2. I wish the *intellectual* training to be limited to reading, writing, arithmetic, and geography.

3. I would have these girls taught to do accurately all domestic work, such as sweeping floors, dusting rooms, scrubbing, bed making, washing and ironing, sewing, mending, and knitting.

4. I would have the trades of dressmaking, millinery, straw-platting, tailoring for men, and such like, taught them.

5. The art of cooking should be made a specialty, and every girl should be instructed in it.

6. In connection with these schools garden plats should be cultivated, and every girl should be required, daily, to spend at least an hour in learning the cultivation of small fruits, vegetables, and flowers.

I am satisfied that the expense of establishing such schools would be insignificant. As to their maintenance, there can be no doubt that, rightly managed, they would in a brief time be self-supporting. Each school would soon become a hive of industry, and a source of income. But the *good* they would do is the main consideration. Suppose that the time of a girl's schooling be limited to *three*, or perchance to *two* years. It is hardly possible to exaggerate either the personal family or society influence which would flow from these schools. Every class, yea, every girl in an outgoing class, would be a missionary of thrift, industry, common sense, and practicality. They would go forth, year by year, a leavening power into the houses, towns, and villages of the Southern black population; girls fit to be thrifty wives of the honest peasantry of the South, the worthy matrons of their numerous households.

I am looking after the domestic training of the MASSES; for the raising up women meet to be the helpers of *poor* men, the RANK AND FILE of black society, all through the rural districts of the South. The city people and the wealthy can seek more ambitious schools, and should pay for them.

Ladies and gentlemen, since the day of emancipation millions of dollars have been given by the generous Christian people of the North for the intellectual training of the black race in this land. Colleges and universities have been built in the South, and hundreds of youth have been gathered within their walls. The work of your own Church in this regard has been magnificent and unrivaled, and the results which have been attained have been grand and elevating to the entire Negro race in America. The complement to all this generous and ennobling effort is the elevation of the black woman. Up to this day and time your noble philanthropy has touched, for the most part, the male population of the South, given them superiority, and stimulated them to higher aspirations. But a true civilization can only then be attained when the life of woman is reached, her whole being permeated by noble ideas, her fine taste enriched by culture, her tendencies to the beautiful gratified and developed, her singular and delicate nature lifted up to its full capacity, and then, when all these qualities are fully matured, cultivated, and sanctified; all their sacred influences shall circle around ten thousand firesides, and the cabins of the humblest freedmen shall become the homes of Christian refinement and of domestic elegance through the influence and the charm of the uplifted and cultivated black woman of the South!

A TRIPLE ALLIANCE FOR THE RESCUE OF A RACE.

By REV. W. V. KELLEY D. D.,

PASTOR OF ST. JOHN'S M. E. CHURCH, BROOKLYN, N. Y.

IN this land of many races there is one race peculiar in its character, history, and lot. Its presence here is explained by reasons far different from those which brought the rest of our population hither. Other elements—English, Irish, Scotch, French, Italian, German, Scandinavian—came here because this is the land of liberty; the Negro was brought here because this was the land of slavery. Unlike the rest of us, the black race is here, not by its own act, but, as has been tersely and truly said, it is here by "the crimes of our ancestors and the misfortunes of its own." Other men came here to obtain their rights; black men came to suffer all the wrongs of man's inhumanity to man. Others found here the privileges of freemen; they found the privations of bondage. Others exulted under "the stars and stripes;" they crouched under scars and stripes.

No other element in the land bears any real resemblance in its lot and experience on American soil. Barbarian, captive, slave, contraband, ward of the nation, freedman, citizen—such is the epitome of its extraordinary history.

It is a race *singular in its service*. The entire wealth of half the land, and no small part of the prosperity of the rest, sprang from his labors. *Singular in suffered outrage*; upon this race, for two centuries, Saxon pride, indolence, luxury, lust, cupidity, and cruelty wreaked their most tyrannous abuse.

Singular in the completeness of its subjection; from first to last it has been permitted no will of its own, but its lot has been created for it.

It was brought here in the beginning against its will, forced over seas and from ship to shore upon our coasts, and off to cotton-field, rice swamp, and cane-brake, "like dumb, driven cattle." It was held here in abject servitude, against its will, under the lash, for two hundred years; set free, not by its own act or power, but by the will of others; made a citizen, and charged with the responsibilities of citizenship, without its knowledge or consent, when it was unfit for such duties. The ballot was thrust into his hands, without the intelligence to use it being provided. This, though logically necessary by the fundamental principles of democracy, was like giving him a dynamite torpedo, which the warmth of his hand would explode, to his own and others' injury.

This race is *singular in the pathos of its story*. Frederika Bremer said that the fate of the Negro is the romance of our history. A race that could not write its name, ignorant even of the alphabet, has been written and spoken about as no other has been, appropriating the most gifted tongues and pens to its cause, and giving occasion to a great body of literature, in prose and poetry, unsurpassed for what is tragic, pathetic, thrilling, and sublime. In all literature there is but one "Uncle Tom's Cabin," and there is no poet dearer to men than Quaker Whittier. So, also, over the lot of this race a tide of *spoken* eloquence has poured forth unmatched in the oratory of the ages for moral grandeur, hot indignation, noble scorn, magnanimity, courage, relentless reasoning, tender appeal, and solemn warning.

This race is *singular in its patience;* illustrating meekness and forbearance in immediate contrast with the arrogance and violence under which it suffered. Provoked beyond all bounds, it has turned its cheek to the smiter, and answered not again—not even when its patience was interpreted as evidence that it had no soul, and was something less than human.

It is *singular in its innocence of any wrong toward others*, in the absence of any ground on which any section or class could make just complaint against it. To-day the North, with a tacit confession of its own complicity, looks on the Negroes, and says, by the lips of ex-President Hayes: "They are the only Americans nowise responsible for slavery or its consequences." And the South, still suffering bitter effects of civil strife, says by the lips of Dr. Calloway, that the freedmen are the only people who had no responsibility for or share in the bringing on of war. So, by the just verdict of all the land, no one has any grievance against them. Under infinite exasperation they have remained innocent of perpetrated wrong, and have come nearer to fulfilling the injunction to love enemies than any other class.

This race is *singular in its faith and hope*. Suffering upon itself the infraction of every just law of heaven or earth, debauched by slavery below the level of all the moralities, kicked down out of sight of virtue, equity, purity, and conscience; yet keeping forever its faith in a God of justice, in the comforts of religion, in the all-seeing eye, in Him who, though he tarry, yet will come; and through lengthening decades of increasing bondage looking confidently for the day of deliverance.

> "Dey know'd de promise nebber fail,
> And nebber lie de word;
> So, like de 'postles in de jail,
> 'Dey waited for de Lord."

And when deliverance came there was more devout and pious thanksgiving in the heart of this despised and ignorant race than could have been found in cultured Athens on "that great morn when Greek salvation broke at Salamis."

This race with this strange record is here, and here to stay; an integral part of the national life, which can not be extirpated or removed. The only element whose fate and treatment bear any resemblance—the red Indian—is disappearing; not so the Negro. In the West, civilization is plowing the savage under, because he will not work; but this man has done the work of half the land for over a century, and now has more and better reasons for working than ever before. He is a factor not to be eliminated, potent, positive, productive, by no means a vanishing quantity. Unquestionably, now and so long as this nation endures, here he is—a fact and a factor.

He is a *fact of our national history*, which we can not ignore, for it involves us as a nation by the record of *wrongs which we have inflicted, and for which we must make amends*. By all good manners and fair equities we owe him an immense apology, couched not in words but deeds, since it is deeds more than words that we have to atone for. It involves us as a nation also by the record of *service we have received and never paid for*. The wages of a hundred years have never been settled. Of this the South owes most, but the whole nation shares in the debt, and the North is far abler to pay than the South. So sure as God lives the people which withholds fair earnings will pay them some way, some day, under writ and exaction from Divine justice. Thus the Negro, whose debtors we are, concerns us as a historic fact, with which we are not done dealing.

He is also a *factor of our national future*. This is not so fully understood, but is important for us to perceive without delay, for it involves every interest of the land.

Consider what a factor he is. He is a *citizen*, a voter, a legislator, a ruler of the land; the vote of the humblest negro in the bayous of the Gulf counts for as much as the vote of General Grant; the humble Louisiana Negro is, therefore, no longer a "low-down, no 'count" person.

Again, the black man *works*, and in a free land the man who works will in the long run possess; he who tills the soil will by and by own it; industry lays its hands on property; property is power; plainly, the working Negro is a man of importance.

Furthermore, the people of color are *increasing;* four millions at close of the war, seven millions now, and there are children alive today who will live to see the colored people in the United States equal in number to the entire present population of the land; within one life-time they are to number fifty millions. This is not prophecy; it is arithmetic, mathematical certainty, worked out on the basis of ascertained facts, by knowing minds. Clearly the Negro is a factor to be taken into account.

When the war ended and liberty reached from the Potomac to the Gulf, the freedmen were nominally free, but largely helpless and in the power of their former masters, homeless, penniless, half-naked, utterly destitute, brutalized by unknown ages of barbarism and two centuries of bondage, and in appalling ignorance. This race, thus crushed and downtrodden, kept by us in darkness in a land of light, held slaves in a country boastful of freedom, God purposed to liberate and uplift. For this work a *triple alliance of forces*, divinely commissioned, has come upon the scene.

Going one afternoon into the house of a colored family among the mountains, I saw on the wall a rifle, on the table two books—a Life of Alfred the Great and a Bible. And I said to myself, these are the fit emblems of the black man's deliverance and elevation.

I looked up at the *rifle*, and remembered the four bloody years which broke the fetters of the slave. I recalled that it was amid the thunder and lightning of an awful war-storm that blindfold Liberty groped through the gloom, along the bastioned walls of slavery, till she found the gates, entered the key of emancipation, shot back the bolts, and set the captives free. The war, which would not have originated without slavery, and which was waged on one side with the avowed intention of founding an empire with slavery for its corner-stone, could not close without the destruction of slavery; and so *War was the first agency* in the rescue of an oppressed race. The decree of emancipation was written by the point of the bayonet as truly as by the point of Lincoln's pen; and so soon as it was signed the armies of the nation massed solid around that fair, just, immortal piece of writing, to make it good, and the roar of rifle, musket, mortar, and cannon broke forth with redoubled determination to thunder down and tire out all gainsaying and opposition. The slave's chains were broken by rifle-balls; of this the rifle on the wall reminded me.

Looking down at the *Life of Alfred the Great*, I remembered that he was the renowned king who is held to this day as the wisest, best, and greatest of England's rulers, and that his chief fame is because, to the lasting benefit of his kingdom, he was the friend and apostle of education. After his wars he found his realm in gross ignorance, especially in its southern part, hardly any body south of the Thames being able to read. He determined to enlighten this ignorance—brought many learned men from afar to help him make books, build centers of education, and diffuse knowledge through his dominions. Thus the great Alfred established in wisdom the strong and magnificent empire which at the end of a thousand years towers in undiminished greatness, and casts the shadow of its power over the whole earth.

Laying my hand on the Life of Alfred, I felt that I held a fit emblem of *Education*, which is *the second great agency* for the uplifting of the Negro.

Beside this volume on the black man's table lay a well worn Bible, the religion of which was dearer to the good Alfred than even education; indeed, he, ten centuries ago, was wise enough to know that the chief value of education is to enable individuals and communities to secure welfare by the intelligent fulfillment of the teachings of God's Word. And the black man's Bible was the symbol and fountain of *Religion*, which is the *third and greatest agency* for the elevation of his race, as of any race.

War has done its work; it remains for education and religion to do theirs. We *must* put the means and appliances of Christian civilization within the reach of the freedmen. *Humanity requires it;* even Seneca said that "man was born for mutual assistance, to stretch his hand to the shipwrecked, show the path to the wanderer, and divide his bread with the hungry." Up to that formula of duty we are to live, or be less Christian than was heathen Seneca. To liberate them, and stop there, would be as if the master of a slave-ship should put his human cargo into small boats and set them adrift in mid-ocean, with no food, water, or clothing, with no means of finding or reaching the far-off land, saying, as he filled his lordly sails and bore away, leaving them helpless: "Now you are free to go where you will and do as you please."

It would be only humane to give them at least a little black bread, a cask of water, something to bale with, and a pair of oars, that they may not sink or die, but have some chance to row ashore. Less than this nobody but a pirate would think of doing.

Simple humanity demands that we give the freedmen the means of self-help.

Public safety requires it, for no republic can live without intelligence and virtue in its citizens. God chains this nation to the task of instructing its own ignorance and uplifting its own depravity; and the nation must do it, or follow the wrecked empires which long ago drove with their dead things down the dark of history. To deny intelligence to citizenhood is to assassinate the republic. If the American people were wise they would compel every child into school, and make education as public as the dust of the highway, which impartially settles alike on the broadcloth of the gentleman and on the sweat-stained shirt of the laborer.

Our national Congress seems insensible to this. Part of the ignorance which needs enlightening and the depravity which needs elevating appears to be in legislative halls.

In the South is a vast mass of illiteracy. When the war closed there were in the sixteen Southern States not more than sixteen schools of any kind on good foundation. A little help was given by Government to the cause of Southern education, through the Freedmen's Bureau, but it was soon withdrawn. Why should not the Government aid education in the South now, as it once did in the West? Eight years ago, at the anniversary of this Society, Dr. Townsend plead, in Washington, for government action. Last Independence Day ex-President Hayes made, with strong reasoning, a like appeal. But such appeals fail to move Congresses, which busy themselves with wasting millions on river and harbor bills, largely bogus, appropriating the treasury surplus ostensibly to make Goose Creek a national water-way, and dredge out mud-puddles for tadpoles to swim in, but really (as the people believe), in many instances, to fill the pockets of pilfering legislators and their friends.

Now, as in Old Testament days, city and nation must be saved by their highest virtue and intelligence; and because we have a plague of politicians and a dearth of statesmen, Christian individuals—like Peabody, Slater, Seney, and Tulane—and the Christian Church must do what Congress is not wise enough nor high enough nor good enough to do.

But education, to insure safety, must reach the moral nature, and be Christian. Fenelon tells us, across two centuries, that "moral education is the bulwark of a State." In Florence, on the triumphal arch erected to Francis II, first Grand Duke of the house of Lorraine, is this inscription: "Religion, uncorrupted, is the public safety." Goldwin Smith has said: "Not democracy in America, but free Christianity in America, is the real key to the study of the people and their institutions." Even Herbert Spencer said, during his visit to this country, last year, that education and diffusion of knowledge alone will not fit men for free institutions; that such fitness is essentially a question of moral character, and only in a secondary degree a question of knowledge; that it is a delusion that education is a panacea; and that it has proved powerless to prevent vice. This is from a man who has been in his day a champion of education, and a discoverer in its science and method. This man warns us that education alone is insufficient. And we say that if a free nation would endure it must combine with its search for the Golden Fleece of prosperity a quest for the Holy Grail of pure religion.

A year and a half ago the preacher who gave the Christmas sermon in the Chapel Royal of St. James' Palace, London, said: "The greatness of the future of nations belongs to the Republic of the United States." Bold words in such place! They can come true only on conditions. So terrible and threatening are the dangers from the lower elements of our population, the ignorant and depraved, that many predict the failure of popular government. Dr. Winchell makes a dark picture in the last February *North American Review;* declares that we go steadily from bad to worse; and implies that our only way of escape from national ruin is to take the ballot out of the hands of the untaught and degraded.

But this can not be. The only glory possible to this land is by carrying out that rule of The All which we call Democracy. We are in for universal suffrage and can not go back. Put in trust with this sublime experiment, we must carry it out. If we fail, after doing our best, it will be failure more glorious than any success yet recorded in history; but it will be the greatest crime possible to be perpetrated by a people if, having been charged with this great enterprise for mankind, we let it drift to failure by stupid and wicked negligence. The continent would not be big enough to dig a grave in which to hide the enormity of our shame.

Launched on the sea of universal suffrage, our great political experiment, freighted deep with the hopes of all the earth will founder and go down with all on board, unless we educate and Christianize, securing intelligence and guarding it by virtue.

To prevent the failure of free institutions no society is doing more than the Freedmen's Aid. With its sixteen years of service, and the educational institutions it has established—numbering now twenty-five—it has done a grand and imperishable work, most of which has been pursued in face of obloquy, contempt, and persecution; nevertheless, bravely, patiently, successfully done.

The education of the Negro has been objected to in some quarters, but the objections are born of prejudice or inhumanity, and when brought together in their best array only make us think of the reasons given by an ancient city council for not cleaning the streets of Madrid. First, it would be a reflection on the wisdom of their ancestors, who had never done it. Second, the air of Madrid was naturally too pure to be wholesome, and needed something to mitigate its excessive purity. Third, the dogs and carrion-birds, which subsisted on the filth and offal, would all starve to death. Fourth, it was an experiment which had never been tried, and no one could tell what disastrous consequences might possibly follow. So the sagacious council decided against cleaning the streets of Madrid.

But objections to such work as this society is doing fall back fast before good results. The best minds of the South now approve. Dr. Haygood bids the South do justice to "our brother in black;" Dr. Calloway begs it to heed the call of "our man of

Macedonia;" both agree that he is ours—not any longer in ownership—but ours to treat brotherly.

The danger, also, of its own illiteracy begins to dawn alarmingly on the wisest men of the South, so that they now show signs of the wisdom which would drain the foul marsh that reeks deadly miasma up into their own windows, or clean the streets of filth which breeds pestilence around their own dwellings.

Dr. Patton, at Howard University, talks of the Negro race as our "American Nazareth," out of which many Nathaniels have declared no good thing could come. The Freedmen's Aid Society triumphantly gives Philip's answer to the doubters—"Come and see."

The question of the black man's capacity is no longer before the house in any intelligent assembly; it has been settled on proof, and is now matter of record.

The freedmen have shown a *thirst for education*. "Their eagerness for the labors of teachers and missionaries has been one of the marvels of the age."

They have shown *ability to master all branches of learning*. They have shown *grateful appreciation* of the self-denying kindness of those who toil among them for their instruction and elevation.

On Lake Maggiore, under the dark-surfaced and shaggy hills of La Gandoglia, are the quarries from which men blast the snowy stone of which they have builded, through seven hundred years, Milan's white marble miracle—a temple filled with stately worship and crowned with figures of saints and angels.

So, under swarthy skins may be found good brain and heart, materials for building many a temple to our God; and as for appreciation, Dr. Rust and his co-laborers have built themselves imperishable monuments out of the white marble quarries of love which lie in black men's hearts.

Against disheartening difficulties, so much has been accomplished that now, when we ask, with our faces southward: "Watchman, what of the night?" Bishop Warren answers, from the center of the dark, "The morning cometh," with more joy than he shouted at sunrise on the Matterhorn or moonrise over the Jungfrau; and Bishop Foster answers, "My conviction is that history furnishes no example of progress equal in the same length of time to that of our colored people in the United States since emancipation. There is vast work yet to be done, for it is a great thing to build up a people from nothing, or worse than nothing; but the result so far is most encouraging."

The work of this society has for its foundation Paul's doctrine of the "one blood." It turns in fear and aversion from the murderer's question, "Am I my brother's keeper?" It hears a Macedonian call, "Come and help us!" It responds with the Crusader's marching-cry, "God wills it!" The spears of its benign warfare are like Jonathan's at Bethaven, "enlighteners of the eyes."

It seeks to provide for the freedmen *teachers of their own race*, to multiply educators in the regions of ignorance. Men do well to call the teacher master. Generals and statesmen do not dignify and ornament or serve their country more than its true teachers. Are there any nobler men in the land than ex-President Woolsey, of Yale, and ex-President Hill, of Harvard, who now is singing sweetest hymns to Christ the Savior, at heaven's gate, while he waits for it to open? The humblest teacher of the freedmen's children is of the same noble brotherhood of educators as they.

This society seeks to provide for the freedmen *preachers of their own race*, that the civilizing Gospel may be preached to them in purity and clearness, under the guidance of the "Spirit of power and of love, and of a sound mind." From this effort I believe great results are to come. A strange and marvelous gift of eloquence belongs to the race, and the South will some day listen to Negro Durbins, Simpsons, Wileys, and Warrens, like and yet different.

Behind the seven millions of Negroes in this country, are the two hundred millions in Africa; and the training-schools of this society will yet furnish missionaries to be fit successors of Carey and Judson, and worthy, in the redemption of the Dark Continent, to lay their bones beside the not whiter bones of Melville Cox and Emma Michener, at Monrovia.

This society seeks to provide for the freedmen *physicians of their own race*, to relieve suffering, heal disease, and inculcate those physical moralities which are conditions of health and virtue.

To make known these facts, and to spread information in such a way as to excite a proper interest in this sublime work, is the object of calling such assemblies as this. It is the strong purpose of faithful and wise men, lovers of God and their country, that neither North nor South shall be allowed to be ignorant of the things which belong to their common peace in this great matter. There is no lack of carefully ascertained, presentable, and impressive facts, no dearth of trustworthy statistics.

At Elberon, by the sea—quaint, lovely, picturesque, Elberon, which was once to all this nation mournful, tragic Elberon—at Elberon, when the railway company was laying a spur off from the line of the road to curve around by the door of the Francklyn cottage, so that the wounded President, who was to be brought from Washington, might be carried as near as possible to the house he would occupy; as they were marking out the curve, the engineer in charge said to the owner of a neighboring cottage, "I'm afraid, sir, we will be obliged to run our track through that flower-bed of yours." And the man full to the lips answered, with the abruptness of intense feeling, "Run it through my house, if you want to."

The cause presented here to-day has better right of way than even the train that bore our murdered chief-magistrate, for a race is greater and more precious than any man. This cause bears not a wounded President, but an injured race, and has unquestionable right of way through our attention, sympathies, prayers, and purses.

If the English sky-lark, who once soared and sang in sun-drenched Italian blue, the "Shakespeare among women," whose pitiful heart wrote "The Cry of the Children," and "The Cry of the Human," and sent to us in faithful love over Western seas, in the days of our disgrace and guilt, "A Curse for a Nation," if she were still on earth, she would find now a new occasion for pleading as once she plead:

> "O gracious Nation! Give some ear to me!
> You all go to your fair, and I am one
> Who at the roadside of humanity
> Beseech your alms—God's justice to be done."

THE METHODIST EPISCOPAL CHURCH IN THE SOUTH.

BY J. M. WALDEN, LL. D.

LESS than twenty years ago the Methodist Episcopal Church opened her *new mission* to the Southern States. I shall speak chiefly of those results which are peculiar to it as a Methodist Episcopal work—characteristic elements and features of this work which spring from the genius of our Connection. But first, of *the Field*, comprising North Carolina, South Carolina, Georgia, Florida, Alabama, Tennessee, Mississippi, Louisiana, Arkansas, and Texas; not of the extent, population, and the like, but of historic facts which impart to our work there a signal interest.

From these ten sovereign Southern States our Church had been practically excluded for twenty years, during which period a generation had grown up from the cradle to manhood and womanhood. Because of this exclusion, I may properly designate it our "new Southern field." We had, however, maintained more than a foothold in the five border States—Delaware, Maryland, Virginia, Kentucky, and Missouri—and were relatively strong in the historic home of Methodism, Baltimore. The numerical force of our Church in 1864, in these five slave States, was 355 effective preachers, 79,069 members (15,898 colored), and 982 church buildings. The Methodist Episcopal Church South shared in the occupancy of these border States, but was the only Methodism in the other ten slave States beyond.

The rupture of the Methodist Church by the secession of 1844-6 had its effect upon the temper and character of the nation as well as upon the parent Church and the seceding body. Wise statesmen of that day contemplated the event with deep concern, and some, with a keener prescience, predicted dangers that would imperil the Union in devotion to which all then vied. The Methodist Episcopal Church South was limited to the slave States (except a Pacific coast work), and embodied the whole of Methodism in ten of these States for more than twenty years, a fact that I can not now stop to trace in its effect upon that Church and the whole people, especially on those since reached by our new work in the South.

Our Church had access to two classes on entering this field, the whites in North Carolina, Tennessee, Georgia, Alabama, Arkansas, and Texas, and the colored people in all of the States from which she had been excluded. The condition of these classes was different. The whites were impoverished by the war, but they had some possessions and some kinds of business; they had church buildings, however dilapidated; but in some places all Church organizations had been disbanded, and in other places the connectional bonds were broken; they were ready, however, for reorganization, and in Eastern Tennessee almost an entire conference (the Holston) voluntarily sought and was given a place among our annual conferences. The colored people had not lost property, for they had none to lose; they had no Church organizations nor buildings, and their Church membership, at best, was only nominal; all they had was their recently proclaimed freedom and their hands trained to toil.

I deem it proper to mention here a fact or two that had some influence on this field and more upon our Church, that was to enter it at an eventful period. However the Church South may have been effected by being limited to the slave States, the maintenance of a work in the border slave States by the Methodist Episcopal Church did have an important influence upon her growth and spirit. It modified the action of every General Conference from that in Pittsburg in 1848 to that in Buffalo in 1860, and this action was the exponent of the conservative temper of the Church, as a whole, while there was enough of the opposite spirit to prevent a general indifference to the great questions involved. Even where little was said in the pulpit in regard to slavery, the public and private prayer for the bondsman and for the Nation was heard at the throne, and the conscience of pastor and people did not, could not, slumber.

This conservatism of our Church had its influence upon the country, and, as we see it now, was it not for good? What would have been the temper of our Church but for the restraints of the border work? and what might have been the temper of the North but for the potential conservatism of a Church that had a pulpit in almost every neighborhood in twenty-five of the States? But for this and kindred influences, among which this was chief, might not the Fugitive Slave Law, the repeal of the

Missouri Compromise, or the invasion of Kansas have been the *causus belli* instead of the assault upon Fort Sumter?

We were disposed to deprecate the neutrality of the border States, but all now see that neutrality was more favorable than secession to the Nation's cause; and no one can weigh the facts without concluding that but for conservative influences in these border States, among which were the presence and power of the Methodist Episcopal Church, the champions of slavery would have carried them into the Confederacy.

I think it might be shown that this conservatism was not unfavorable to the preparation of our Church for the special work in the South, to which she was to be called. In suggesting some manifest advantages of this conservatism to the Church and to our country, I do it as one who had little sympathy with it, for when but a boy I felt that the area of slave territory ought not to be increased by the annexation of Texas, and from the time of shameful compromises in 1850 to the time when the Nation rejoiced that four million fetters had been melted in the fires of war, I believed that no concession could be made to slavery without a corresponding peril to freedom.

While our Church was barely maintaining her hold in the border slave States she was developing her activity and strength, and maturing all connectional agencies through efforts to do her part in the evangelization of the rapidly growing West and Northwest. The missionary contributions, which in 1845 amounted to $94,562.27, reached in 1865 $642,740.67. The appropriations to mission work within the United States in 1865 amounted to $254,675, an increase of fivefold during the twenty years. Feeble missions had grown into annual conferences, and the working power of the Church was unprecedented. Strange to say, that at this juncture the treasury of our Missionary Society contained a surplus of nearly $500,000, and had as assistant Corresponding Secretary—though the Corresponding Secretary in fact—the honored president of this meeting (Bishop Harris), who had been elected to that position in 1860 by the advanced party in the General Conference. He was in hearty sympathy with our new work in the Southern States and recognized its importance.

Such was the field and such the preparation of our Church to enter it. Can any one doubt that she was appointed and called to this work by her Living Head? During the seventeen years an increasing corps of laborers has been employed in the ten States; $1,400,000 have been expended by the Missionary Society; $1,250,000 by the Freedmen's Aid Society; the Board of Church Extension has aided in the erection of 936 church buildings, besides what has been done by the Sunday-school Union and the Tract Society. With what result? Within these ten States, at the close of 1882, there were 20 annual conferences, 737 effective traveling preachers, 2,185 church buildings, 156,116 Church members (41,389 white and 114,727 colored), not including 26,057 probationers, all the result of seventeen years of work.

The numerical force of our Church in 1863, in the five border States (six since the partition of Virginia), was 332 effective preachers, 76,670 Church members (not including 8,003 probationers), and 919 church buildings. In 1882, it had increased to 852 effective preachers (224 colored), 190,015 Church members (48,334 colored), not including 29,632 probationers, and 2,435 church buildings — making in the sixteen Southern States an aggregate of 1,589 effective preachers (732 colored), 346,131 Church members (163,061 colored), 55,689 probationers (26,499 colored), and 4,620 church buildings, valued at about seven millions of dollars—an actual increase of 1,157 effective preachers, 269,461 Church members, 47,686 probationers, and 3,701 church buildings in the eighteen years.

Such is one view of what the Methodist Episcopal Church has done in the South, a view that might be made even more striking by a fuller presentation of the facts. I wish, however, to speak of other results, which are less obvious but more important—the effect of this work on the people for whose benefit it has been done, the effect of planting our Methodism among them, with its polity and connectional agencies, its doctrinal teachings, religious spirit, and moral power.

1. The number of preachers from the North has been less than would be supposed from the antagonism awakened or from the results achieved. The demand was not for a numerous band of missionaries, but for leaders, for men who could promptly organize and prudently direct a new work. The bishops selected a few men, some of whom had learned much concerning the new field while in their country's service, to aid them in organizing and superintending the work. Among these were James F.

Chalfant, D. D., A. A. Gee, D. D., and Rev. A. S. Lakin, in the Central South; Rev. W. T. Lewis and A. Webster, D. D., in South Carolina and Florida; John P. Newman, D. D., and Rev. N. L. Brakeman, in Louisiana; Rev. A. C. McDonald, in Mississippi; J. D. Mitchell, D. D., and James Mitchell, D. D., in North Carolina and Virginia; Rev. Joseph Welch, in Texas. And these were soon joined by John Braden, D. D., Thomas H. Pearne, D. D., David Rutledge, D. D., J. F. Spence, D. D., E. Q. Fuller, D. D., L. C. Matlack, D. D., N. C. Cobleigh, D. D., J. C. Hartzell, D. D., Rev. J. J. Manker, Rev. S. B. Darnell, E. Cooke, D. D., and a few others. Of the seven hundred and thirty-seven effective preachers now within the "new Southern field," nearly seven hundred are native, "to the manor born."

A proper estimate of the work done in this field can not be made without a clear view of the condition of the peoples who have been reached and benefited. Civilized society never before presented such a scene as our missionaries found in the South. The people everywhere were impoverished; every industry was paralyzed; the social order that had molded many generations was broken up; the relation of master and slave had ceased to be, but both parties to this relation were still there; the exhaustion of war alone prevented general disorder becoming lawlessness. Into this scene our Church was called; into it, at her bidding, her heroes went.

Picture to yourselves for the moment those to whom our Church found an open door—the impoverished and almost churchless white people, and the colored people, who were not only without homes, but without the relations of the home; not only without earthly possessions, but impoverished in the best elements of their nature. It may be no marvel that societies were soon gathered and conferences soon organized among the whites, for with them it was chiefly a work of reorganization and edification. But what of the work among the freed people—those who had only toiled as house-servants and slave-mechanics and field-hands. Here, among them, the very foundations of Church-work had to be laid, and our first movement in this direction—the necessary and the right movement—was to give them, at once, their normal relation in and to the Church. The records of Methodism in America would show colored members almost from the beginning; a colored membership was recognized and reported by the Methodist Episcopal Church South; but there were no colored congregations and charges with pastors taken from among themselves, and no colored minister had a place of equality in the conferences which reported that membership. I do not discuss here the obvious causes of these facts, but only state the facts as they bore upon our work in that "new Southern field."

So far as I know, in every mission district formed in all this field, colored preachers promptly received authority from the Methodist Episcopal Church to carry the Gospel to their people, and when these districts were superseded by annual conferences these colored men had their equal place in them, and no thought of any other relation for them was ever entertained, much less mooted. As the work grew the creation of new conferences became expedient, and authority was given by the General Conference for a separation into white and colored bodies, on principles that recognized the Christian and ministerial equality of all the members. It would be interesting to trace and study the molding influence of our Methodism on the eight white conferences now found in the "new Southern field;" but as my time is limited, I direct your thought to that influence on and within the other twelve conferences, comprising the people among whom the Freedmen's Aid Society has done its grandest work.

2. Wherever the Methodist Episcopal Church plants a mission she carries with her her Itineracy and its auxiliary agencies, her connectional benevolences, and her aggressive, evangelical spirit. I greatly desire to lead your thought in grouping the results of this triplet of forces among the freed people, who less than twenty years ago had neither a ministry nor a Church in any true sense. The superintendents of the mission districts found colored men who were called to preach; but under the slave system, from which they had just been delivered, they had not been able to qualify themselves for the work of the ministry, and none of them had been formally set apart to that work.

Two courses were open—one to delay employing colored preachers until they could be educated; the other, to put these untutored men to work at once. No people ever needed the Gospel more than did the freed people. Standing in the midst of new relations, the possessors of a new-found freedom for which they had never been trained, they needed both the restraints and the inspiration of the Gospel. The Wesleyan prescience of our Church recognized this need, and at the same time the fact that these unlearned preachers, if divinely called, could so tell the story of the Cross as to benefit their people. The lives of many of these men had been an unbroken period of slave-toil; but the sequel proves that they knew enough of the saving power of Christ and the fullness of his love to instruct their hearers in the way of life, and we now see that their relation to this work was not unlike to that of the first of Wesley's lay preachers to their work among their own classes in England.

Of other denominations that saw the open door to the freed people, and heard the Master's call in behalf of his most needy ones, some believed that a ministry should be raised up among them by proper education. However desirable an education may be, our Church could not stay her work for the ex-slave to attend the schools. In judging of the two methods, the mention of results can not be regarded as invidious. The American Missionary Association, in these ten States, has gathered into Churches from this people 4,961 members; the Presbyterian Freedmen's Union has gathered 11,108 members,—while our Church has, in the same territory, among the same people, 114,727 members and 20,733 probationers.

With this illustration before us of the general principle that a people may and must be instrumental in their own evangelization, let us study some of the results of our itinerant system among the freedmen—of our Itinerancy and its auxiliary agencies. All understand our Itinerancy to be the general superintendency and the pastorate; by auxiliary agencies I mean our sub-pastorate in which the class-leaders stand, our Church literature, and our Sunday-schools. The mere suggestion of the fact leads you at once to see that the real function of each and all of these is to re-enforce both the general and the particular work committed to the Itinerancy or three-fold pastorate—the bishops, presiding elders, and pastors of our Church. The very fact of taking this comprehensive system to a people who had no system, of beginning at once to build them up into it, could not be without producing some marked and favorable results. I mention the more obvious of these:

(*a*) The freedmen who were recognized as having a call to preach could do little more than exhort, but they were put into the pastoral relation; a great Church committed to them a new and solemn trust, and laid upon them grave responsibilities; they were under the leadership of the superintendents of the missions—good, prudent, self-sacrificing men—men who in their devotion to duty represented the highest life of their Church. Such things could not be without affecting these untutored preachers. Crude as all they did may have been at first, their pastorate benefited the people they served, and was to themselves a means of training, of real and rapid progress; and there are still in the effective ranks of the conferences which came from such beginnings many pious, able, and successful preachers, who were thus transferred from the cotton and rice fields and sugar plantations to, and trained in, our itinerant ministry.

(*b*) As the work progressed, these colored men acquired by observation and experience, and such study as was possible with them, a wider knowledge of their work; and in due course the bishops began to appoint some of them as presiding elders, investing them with all the honors and responsibilities of this important office. It should also be stated that the Church that acted thus through her bishops was constantly displaying to them an encouraging interest in them by furnishing means to aid in the support of their Church work.

(*c*) In the annual conferences they were and are brought under the presidency of our bishops—the most efficient presiding officers in this or any other country, a fact that became most obvious at the Ecumenical Methodist Conference. The very methods of business in our annual conferences, and the promptness with which it is dispatched under this presidency, have had such influence on the older conferences that the advantages of like administration to the colored conferences are obvious. The influence of the conference session ought also to be named, as these annual meetings of the preachers have all along affected most favorably the character of Methodism. These colored preachers have been coming together, as do their brethren in older conferences, to report and review the year's work, to pass upon the character of each one, to consider the various connectional and benevolent causes, to attend to all the business that is usually presented, and to enjoy the social privileges and religious services to which all our preachers look forward with deep interest. Every such session tends to make them wiser and more effective in their work.

(d) Under our system of study for probationers and deacons, the colored preachers are steadily improving, and their conferences are becoming more careful as to the qualifications of those who are received into the ministry. I well remember the class taken on trial in the South Carolina Conference in 1867; near a dozen of them were then uncouth and ill-clad men, who seemed to have come direct from the plantations; little or nothing was said as to even elementary education; they were taken as they were, and sent out to do work for the Master who ordaineth strength even out of the mouths of babes. But it is radically different in that conference now; at its session, last January, I heard the report of examinations, and learned thereby that the standard of qualification is applied more rigidly each succeeding year. I rejoiced in this as a fact common to all these colored conferences, and yet I also rejoiced to remember that when the exigencies required it our Church dared to send out the earlier members of that and other conferences, illiterate as they were, to the work of winning souls.

(e) These early colored preachers, coming as they did from a condition in which there was no home, in the better sense of that word, soon came to know something of the importance that our Church attaches to Sunday-schools. They were organized, often, in the crudest form, but they have been improved, and now nearly two thousand are reported in the twelve conferences. This work is important there, not only because it is in behalf of the youth and children, but also because there has been and is a relatively great demand for such work in the South. It is a fact that the ratio between the number of Sunday-school scholars and Church members of any and all Protestant denominations in the South is far below what it is in the North. The schools organized in our "new Southern field" have been aided with papers published by our Church, and especially adapted to the condition of the scholars. All the teachers employed by the Freedmen's Aid Society have done good and faithful service in these Sunday-schools. Through them the Church has been and is furnishing moral and mental instruction to about one hundred thousand of the youth and children, that will be of incalculable value to them, and through them to the Church and the Nation.

(f) The Methodist newspapers published in the South—within this new field—by our Church, in order to furnish a literature specially adapted to the condition and needs of the people, have been potent for good. We may not be able to estimate the force of the fact that papers have been provided for them which they in a special sense regarded as their own. It was no mean fact with them that a part of the capital of the Book Concern was being employed to publish papers which by their very location must chiefly be for them. And the presence of a Depository of Books at Atlanta tended to impress the lesson, taught in so many ways, that our Church was ready and anxious to help them in their every effort to reach the plane of a higher and better life.

Other facts might be named to show how every thing that is forceful in our Itinerancy and its auxiliary agencies has been constantly, wisely, and effectively employed to reach, evangelize, and elevate these colored people. It has been more than a formal recognition of Christian equality; it has been the continuous presence and power of educational relations as well as educational agencies among them. The Church, during these years, has recognized the divine call into her ministry of more than a thousand of these men, thereby reposing a confidence and conferring an honor that has been a special inspiration to them and, in good degree, to their people. Ministerial position and pastoral duties, prerogatives and responsibilities, shared in common with the largest corps of preachers in our country have been made realities to them. When that whole people shall come to the plane and glory of a true manhood and womanhood, it will be known that the impartial planting of our system of itinerancy among them was one of the early and potent means of their elevation.

3. The aim of the Methodist Episcopal Church is to enlist every local society in the support of her benevolent enterprises. She would give to every person converted at her altars the opportunity to do work for the Master. For this reason, all her pastors are charged with the duty of presenting to their congregations the claims of the Missionary, Church Extension, Freedmen's Aid, Sunday-school, Tract, and Educational causes, and of affording to all the opportunity to contribute thereto according to their ability. Into each sphere of work represented by these causes, the Church has been led by a marked providence, and her efforts in them have been attended with her Lord's signal favor. The presentation of these causes in the relation they hold to the world's evangelization, the end for which Christ established his Church, teaches

with special emphasis the magnitude of her mission, and indicates the certainty of ultimate success. How the faith of God's people has enlarged under the inspiration of this widening work! These causes have been presented more or less fully to our new societies in the South.

The colored preachers and people have taken a ready interest in the Missionary Society because it carried the Gospel to them. The preachers were not learned, and the people were poor—but what if the earlier missionary sermons were crude presentations of a world-wide cause? what if but a few pennies were collected in a charge? the people were thus coming into contact with the genius of the Gospel, and beginning to have some part in the movement that is conquering the world. Among the many wise things done during the administration of the revered Dr. Durbin as Missionary Secretary, the one of all others that has affected and will continue to affect our Church the most was providing for the organization of the Sunday-schools into missionary societies; wise and potential, because thus in a practical and methodical way the idea of the world's evangelization is fixed in the thought of the youth and children, by far the greatest idea touching the human race that can be given to the human mind.

The colored preachers have been learning this fundamental idea of the missionary cause and the purpose of each of the other benevolences of our Church, and in their own way it may be presenting them to their people; but the result has been a measure of enlightenment in these directions, an increasing knowledge of the far-reaching plans of the Church to which they belong, a clearer consciousness that by being brought within her pale they have part in one of the great aggressive Christian movements of the age. Standing as they do in the dawn of a new day, this conscious identification with all the benevolent plans of the Church that brought them the Gospel can not do less than enlarge their views of Christian duty, and inspire them with zeal for and devotion to causes grand in themselves and glorious in their results.

4. The preaching that is distinctively Methodistic has had its influence in this as in other fields. While we hold the fundamental truths of Christianity in common with other evangelical Churches—points of agreement each of which is infinitely more important than all the questions in regard to which there is a difference—all do not place the same emphasis we do on some

of these truths. Our preachers in the "new Southern field," as elsewhere, have given special prominence to the willingness and power of Jesus to save every one who comes to Him; the universal call and the gracious ability of every one to come; the radical character of the change wrought in conversion—a new life through divine power; the adoption into the divine Family and that adoption clearly, satisfactorily, attested through the witness of the Holy Spirit; the complete cleansing power of the Blood of Christ and the keeping power of the promised grace. Need I say in this presence that the emphasis given to these Scriptural doctrines by our ministry has molded the experience of Methodists in every society, and made the meeting for testimony, whether love-feast or class-meeting, a part of our Church life. The preaching of these doctrines in the earnest Methodist way among the colored people, the building up of a Church among them under the molding and inspiring effect of such truths, the leading of the members up to a clear, well-defined religious experience, is giving them a Church life the advantage of which is best known from what Methodism has done for other peoples. Already the advance of Christian morality, the growing habits of industry and economy, the increasing spirit of benevolence and liberality, the new home-life where home was so recently unknown—the fruits of an evangelical Gospel faithfully preached—show what we have done, and are the promise and pledge of a pure, strong, and active Church in every part of our new Southern field in the near future.

5. Besides all the agencies comprised in this missionary work, our Church has also gone to the Freed people with the means of education. She did not begin her school-work among them so early as other denominations, chiefly—I may say, solely—because of a sentiment favorable to the undenominational societies by which schools were begun among the "contrabands" early in 1863, and maintained for several years. After, however, other leading denominations had withdrawn from the undenominational work, and the need of schools in our Mission Conferences became imperative, even so late as 1866, the Freedmen's Aid Society, whose anniversary we celebrate, was formed. I could speak of the whole work from an official connection with it for more than twenty years—first with the undenominational Freedmen's Aid Commissions, and then with our own Freedmen's Aid Society. I will only refer to the satisfaction I now have in the fact that during the first

three years I issued commissions to nearly four hundred teachers and other benevolent workers among the freedmen. I do rejoice most heartily in the grand and conspicuous achievements of others in these later years, while I am grateful to God that he gave me, with LEVI COFFIN and other life-long friends of the colored man, an active part in the earlier and foundation work.

Yonder I see, herded together in a "corral," the Contrabands, a mixed and half-clad multitude of all ages, barely kept from famishing by stinted rations; under a tree or shed near by are children, youth, and older ones, pressing around the fair, sweet-faced teacher whose soul is absorbed in her blessed work. Angels seldom have had so grand a mission—they never ministered with a purer motive. The names of a thousand such heroines might be given, and ought to be preserved. Twenty years sweep by; the Contraband is almost forgotten, but a Freed people, with their homes and their industries, are a part of our Nation; and instead of the school of the "corral" are college buildings of the best style of architecture, school-rooms with many appliances and facilities, and corps of experienced teachers, true-hearted Christian men and women. The school in the "corral" was first opened twenty years ago last January; to-day the school property owned by our Freedmen's Aid Society alone has cost about $450,000. I have not time to speak of the work of these twenty years—a benevolent work that is already affecting in most wholesome ways the condition of our country, and will entail benefits that are far-reaching and immeasurable.

6. My theme requires me to say that the Methodist Episcopal Church reached the South through the Freedmen's Aid Commissions long before she had a Freedmen's Aid society of her own. I speak from official knowledge when I say that by far the larger proportion of all union meetings, at which contributions were received for the general work, were held in Methodist Episcopal churches. This was especially true in States west of the Alleghanies, where the movement seemed to have the widest favor of the people. Most denominations were represented among the teachers and other workers; not a few of them were Methodists. It is due the entire corps to say that their fellowship was never shadowed, their work never marred, by a sectarian spirit. Those few years of united effort among the Churches form a bright era in the history of Christian benevolence; it was the best form for the

turbulent times of war, but was succeeded by forms better adapted to the new conditions of after years.

The careful and comprehensive Report of our Freedmen's Aid Society submitted by its Corresponding Secretary, the veteran educator, Rev. Dr. Rust, shows the extent and character of the educational work of our Church in her new Southern field. The number of institutions established, the number of school-buildings erected, the number of teachers employed, the number of pupils instructed during the past sixteen years, are matters of great moment, not only to the people benefited, but to our whole people. These results might be studied with interest; but I wish the rather to keep before you the thought of our Church, of which the Freedmen's Aid Society and all its agencies are the outgrowth and visible embodiment.

Through the formal recognition of this Society by the General Conference, and its adoption by our people as the almoner of their gifts, our Church acknowledged and asserted the right of the ex-slaves and their children to education. In the first General Conference after the close of the war, the thought of more than a million Methodists was voiced thus: "Through the overthrow "of slavery God in his providence has opened before our Church "an extended and unparalleled field of usefulness in the South, "to the cultivation of which we are impelled by the strongest "convictions of duty, and by every humane, patriotic, and Chris- "tian sentiment, and a field where the school and the Church "must be planted together, and the minister and teacher must "labor side by side."

Statutes enacted under the stress of reconstruction, after the close of the war, formally established the right of the colored people to educational privileges, but law is slow in transforming public opinion; the rising sentiment in the South in favor of schools for all is attributable not so much to forms of law as to the moral influence of the presence of schools for the colored people maintained by Northern benevolence; and, both because of their location and their connectional relation, no schools have been more potential in favorably affecting public opinion in the South than those planted and maintained by our Church through the agency of her own Freedmen's Aid Society.

Our Church has also recognized the possibilities connected with education, and plainly and faithfully interpreted them. She has acted in view of the fact that education is the highway to the learned professions as well as to all business pursuits that require trained minds, and that colored men and women, when qualified, ought to have unquestioned access to them. Some pupils who showed a special aptitude were encouraged by the Freedmen's Aid Commissions to prepare themselves for teaching; but the *leading and avowed object* of our Freedmen's Aid Society was to prepare its pupils for *teaching* and *preaching*—to help them into the two professions that do most for social and civil advancement. This object awakened the interest and enlisted the sympathy of our people in the North, and it was soon impressed on our people in the South by the provisions in our schools among them for Normal and Biblical instruction and training. Primary instruction had to be given; but its preparatory relation was kept distinctly in view, so that even the pupils who had no thought of either teaching or preaching were impressed with the advanced character of these callings for which their associates were being prepared.

The next step was the inauguration of a Medical Department in the Central Tennessee College, from which a few young colored men have graduated and begun to practice, having by successful study won their place in a learned profession to which admission is most carefully guarded. Already a leading physician, one of long standing in Nashville, has enlisted his profession in establishing a medical library for this school. The medical students prosecute their studies under the *régime* of a Methodist college, and they go forth as Christian men to a professional life among their people. During all these years through which our Church has labored to secure equal privileges to the colored people, what has she done that can be more effective than planting this pioneer medical school, thereby opening the way to this honorable and most useful profession?

The thought of our Church in regard to the colored people—her clear perception of the condition in which freedom found them, her enthusiastic hope as to what they would become through religion and culture, and her profound conviction of duty on her own part—this thought of our Church, embodied in the Freedmen's Aid Society and interpreted by its plans and work, has given to her missionary movements in the entire South that tone, character, force, and adaptation which has been fruitful in the important results of which I have already spoken. That the present status of this work is not solely what the officers of the Church and her various societies have made it, but is the outgrowth and embodiment of the thought of the Church, is clearly seen in the action of the General Conference, whose wise and world-embracing plans are the exponent of her intelligence, her conscience, her faith, and her fervent spirit.

The General Conference of 1864 met long enough after the Proclamation of Emancipation to see and understand the opportunity afforded by the removal of all legal restrictions to missionary and educational work among the freed people; in the presence of the broader field thus opened and the higher duty imposed, and with petitions from colored members and colored local preachers for advanced legislation, there was significance in the declaration: "As a Church we have never sought, do not "now seek to ignore our duty to the colored population." A Committee on the State of the Work among the People of Color, appointed on the third day of the session, after more than two weeks' deliberation, submitted a report based on "direct informa-"tion from delegates to the General Conference familiar with the "work; from intelligent and trustworthy local preachers who "have been deputed by the colored charges in Delaware, Mary-"land and the District of Columbia to represent them before the "Committee; and from various memorials setting forth the wishes "of our colored members." The twofold plea was for a colored pastorate and conference organization. Neither the memorialists nor the General Conference at first realized the providential bearing of these petitions. As the widening field, still darkened with the smoke of battle, was studied, the possible achievements of a free Gospel in it were perceived, and its occupation thus suggested: "If it be a principle patent to Christian enterprise that "the missionary field itself must produce the most efficient mis-"sionaries, our colored local preachers are peculiarly important "to us at this time. With these properly marshaled, what hin-"dereth that we go down and possess the land?" I wish to emphasize the fact that they were "our local preachers,"—in 1856 they and other colored office-bearers were established in their official relation to the Quarterly Conference of our Church.

After careful deliberation—after a report on the educational work among the Freedmen had been considered and adopted, and thus every phase of the question was in mind—the General

Conference provided for a colored pastorate by means of colored conferences, as follows:

"1. *Resolved*, By the General Conference of the Methodist Episcopal Church in conference assembled, that it is the duty of our Church to encourage *colored pastorates* for *colored people* wherever practicable, and to contribute to their efficiency by every means in our power.

"2. *Resolved*, That the efficiency of said pastorates can be best promoted by distinct conference organizations, and that therefore the bishops be and they are hereby authorized to organize among our colored ministers, for the benefit of our colored members and population, Mission Conferences—one or more—where in their godly judgment the exigencies of the work may demand it; and should more than one be organized, to determine their boundaries until the meeting of the next General Conference, said conference or conferences to possess all the powers usual to Mission Annual Conferences. *Provided*, that nothing in this resolution be so construed as to impair the existing constitutional rights of our colored members on the one hand, or to forbid, on the other, the transfer of white ministers to said Conference or Conferences where it may be practicable and deemed necessary.

"3. *Resolved*, That our General Missionary Committee be requested to take into careful consideration the condition of our colored people, and should Conferences be organized among them, make to them—consistently with other demands upon its funds—such appropriations as may be essential to success."—*Journal*, 1864, *pp.* 252-3.

Before the close of the session the provisional work referred to the bishops was remanded to a special committtee, a report from which was adopted by the General Conference, by defining the boundaries of the Delaware and Washington Conferences, and suspending the probationary rule of two years, so as to allow the bishops to organize into such Mission Conferences the colored elders who had traveled two years under presiding elders, and were properly recommended. [Journal, 1864, p. 263.] The important action of 1864 concerning this work was crowned with this declaration: "We are not aware of any legal obstacle to the reception "of colored preachers into our Annual Conferences;" a declaration that prepared the way for the so-called "mixed conferences."

The bishops, four years later, in their address to the General Conference of 1868, thus reported the results of organizing the Delaware and Washington Colored Conferences:

"They now contain one hundred and one ministers, and twenty-six thousand four hundred and eighty-seven members and probationers. The creation of these conferences was hailed, by our colored ministers and membership, with great joy, and has, we believe, been productive of much good. The ministers are becoming familiar with the mode of conducting business, and many of them are rapidly improving. At their recent sessions they elected representatives to this body, according to the form of the Discipline for electing delegates. Whether these representatives should be admitted you alone have authority to decide. In our judgment, the success of this work demands all the encouragement which the General Conference can properly give."

The first thing the General Conference did to encourage this work was to invest its two colored Mission Conferences with the full powers of Annual Conferences, giving to their delegates a constitutional place in its own body, making them equal in privilege and prerogative with the delegates of other Annual Conferences, thereby providing all the conditions of their perpetuation as colored Conferences.

The quadrennium that had just closed was one of signal importance to our Southern work. The bishops had organized nine Mission Conferences in what I have designated as our "new Southern field," and a fresh impulse was given our work in the Border States. Colored preachers were received into the Kentucky and Missouri Annual Conferences, and in 1867 a colored presiding elder was appointed to one of the colored districts in Kentucky. Most, if not all, of the Southern Mission Conferences were at first or soon became mixed. Many of the white preachers were Southern men, yet there was no hesitancy in according to their colored co-laborers the rights and recognition of brethren. Here was Christian heroism! Only those who can understand the force of long-standing social views, and the depth of feelings even unconsciously engendered by an established social order, will form a full estimate of the devotion to Christian principle displayed by our native Southern white preachers who voted colored preachers into conference relations with themselves.

This General Conference provided for another colored Annual Conference in the Border States by authorizing a division of the Kentucky Conference in this resolution:

"*Resolved*, That the bishops who may preside in the Kentucky Conference, at any time within the next four years, are hereby authorized to organize the colored ministers within the bounds of said Conference into a separate Annual Conference if said ministers request it, and if, in the judgment of the bishops, the interests of the work require it, to be called the ―― Conference; *provided*, that nothing in this resolution shall be construed to impair the existing constitutional rights of our colored members, on the one hand, or, on the other, to prevent the transfer of white ministers to said Conference whenever it may be deemed desirable or expedient."—*Journal*, 1868, *p*. 318.

This General Conference gave to the Southern work a large share of attention. A most important question presented for consideration at the opening of the session was the relation the delegates from the Southern Mission Conferences should hold, and if any members had come to Chicago indifferent as to our new work in the South their interest in it was awakened by the discussions in regard to seating those delegates. The restrictions were taken from the conferences, including the two colored Conferences, by a yea and nay vote of 197 to 15; two Standing Committees presented carefully prepared reports upon different phases of the work; its peculiar difficulties and special wants were considered; its magnitude, importance, and claim on the Church were emphasized; all our benevolent societies were directed to give special attention to its needs; the Book Concerns were ordered to publish one or more papers adapted to its wants; the transfer of ministers required by the work was recommended; "the maintenance "of training and theological schools in the South" for the preparation of teachers and preachers was commended to the cooperation of our whole Church [Journal, 1868, pp. 266-9]; it was further declared that "the educational interests of the white "and colored people should be promoted by liberal and timely "aid;" and even the demand for more of direct episcopal service was recognized. [Journal, 1868, pp. 562-4.] Subsequently the enabling act for the third colored Conference, already mentioned, was adopted, in which a proviso was carefully inserted which implied that in the mind of that General Conference the rights of every preacher had been fully conserved.

During the succeeding quadrennium the rapid growth of our Church among the colored people enlisted much interest, and led to a wide discussion of the measures that would add to the effectiveness of the work. One of the questions that came up in advance of the General Conference of 1872 was the election of a colored bishop, and it was brought before that body at an early day through memorials from a few of the Southern Conferences. The Committee on Episcopacy, composed of a delegate from each Annual Conference, to which these memorials were referred, presented a report, by the adoption of which the General Conference put this declaration before the world:

"There is nothing in race, color, or former condition that is a bar to an election to the Episcopacy, the true course being for us to elect only such persons as are, by their pre-eminent piety, endowments, culture, general fitness, and acceptability, best qualified to fill the office."—*Journal*, 1872, p. 252.

In response to a memorial subsequently received from the Preachers' Association of New Orleans, the General Conference referred to the declaration already made, and further affirmed:

"Election to the office of bishop from among candidates who are mutually equals can not be determined on the ground of color or any other special consideration. It can only be by fair and honorable competition between the friends of the respective candidates."—*Journal*, 1872, p. 373.

The first memorial presented to this General Conference in regard to our colored work came from the Georgia Annual Conference, praying for the organization of a colored Conference. This was accompanied with a petition for the same thing from a convention of the colored members of that Conference, in which they advanced nine reasons for giving them a separate Conference, of which the following were of a general character:

"1. It will enable us to demonstrate our capacity for self-government, by imposing on us the responsibilities of self-government.

"2. It will secure greater efficiency in the prosecution of the work in this State among both white and colored.

"3. It will relieve us from the taunts and sneers of designing men, and secure the communion and friendship of many who would not otherwise unite with us.

"7. It will relieve the Church of even a suspicion of a spirit of caste, and make us feel as men, and the peers of our white brethren.

"8. It will be no innovation upon any principle of Christianity or of our beloved Church, but simply a reiteration of the principle evinced in the organization of the four German Conferences, and the Washington, Delaware, and Lexington Conferences."—*Journal*, 1872, pp. 92-94.

These papers went to the Committee on Boundaries. Several memorials against the creation of colored Conferences were received, chiefly from South Carolina and Louisiana; they were referred to the same Committee, but none of them were spread upon the Journal. This Committee made but one recommendation, which was adopted, as follows:

"*Resolved*, That the Missouri and St. Louis Conferences be permitted to organize, during the next four years, a Conference to include the States of Missouri and Kansas; *provided*, a majority of the colored ministers of these Conferences desire it and the bishops presiding concur."—*Journal*, 1872, *p*. 427.

It seems certain that this General Conference did not consider either its provisional creation of one colored Conference or its declining to create or authorize another an improper discrimination in favor of or against any locality or any part of the Church; and especially in view of its emphatic declarations of the broad principles of Christian equality, its course can only be imputed to a proper and careful regard for the interests of the whole Church—as much for those of her colored as of her white preachers and members.

The question of dividing certain Conferences in the Southern work came before the General Conference of 1876 by memorials and petitions. The Committee on the State of the Church, composed of one delegate from each Annual Conference, forty-eight ministers and thirty-two laymen, submitted a report upon the question, which states:

"The Committee have, by a large sub-committee, given much time to its consideration, and have investigated carefully the matter referred to them. They have considered the numerous memorials, petitions, and resolutions presented to the General Conference on the subject, whether from Annual Conferences, conventions, or private individuals. They have consulted with most, if not all, the delegates to the General Conference, who represent Conferences particularly interested in the question of division, and have studied the history of the movements in several Conferences seeking to effect or prevent division within a few years past, and report the following result of its investigation."

Then follows a concise yet full statement of the reasons, pro and con, with this conclusion:

"From these facts, and after impartially inquiring into the whole subject, your Committee recommend for adoption the following resolutions:

"*Resolved*, 1. That where it is the general desire of the members of an Annual Conference that there should be no division of such Conference into two or more Conferences in the same territory; and where it is not clearly to be seen that such division would favor or improve the state of the work in any Conference; and where the interests and usefulness of even a minority of the members of such Conference, and of the members of Churches in such Conference, might be damaged or imperiled by division, it is the opinion of this General Conference that such division should not be made.

"*Resolved*, 2. That whenever it shall be requested by a majority of the white members, and also a majority of the colored members, of any Annual Conference that it be divided, then it is the opinion of this General Conference that such division should be made, and in that case the bishop presiding is hereby authorized to organize the new Conference or Conferences."—*Journal*, 1872, *pp.* 329–331.

The last resolution differs in form from the original report, but was adopted by a yea and nay vote—226 yeas and 66 nays; the first affirmative vote was given by a colored delegate; only fourteen of the sixty-seven delegates from Conferences in the South voted in the negative.

This action was followed immediately by instructions to the Committee on Boundaries to divide the Georgia and Alabama Conferences, as requested in petitions from them.

One principle running through this legislation of the four General Conferences is that in the creation of new Conferences the rights of the colored members must be guarded; the proviso and declaration adopted in 1864, and reiterated in 1868, is the same in effect as the rule of 1876 under which Conferences have since been divided; all through the legislation and administration there has been a well-defined recognition of the Christian and ecclesiastical equality among the members of an Annual Conference. The true interpretation of the declarations, provisos, and rules adopted by these several and consecutive General Conferences seems to be that in the judgment of the Church the election of any officer on the ground of race or color, or the creation of colored Conferences when and where the interest and work of the Church would be best served by mixed Conferences, or the continuation of mixed Conferences where separate organizations would best promote her work of reaching, elevating, and saving the people, are to be alike avoided. This interpretation is better voiced by the General Conference itself in these weighty words:

"There is no word 'white' to discriminate against race or color known in our legislation; and being of African descent does not prevent membership with white men in Annual Conferences, nor ordination at the same altars, nor appointment to Presiding Eldership, nor election to the General Conference, nor eligibility to the highest offices in the Church."—*Journal*, 1872, *p.* 373.

It is just nineteen years since the first colored Conference—the Delaware—was organized (July 28, 1864). We now have fourteen colored and three mixed Conferences, not including two in Kansas, a Northern State. Into these nineteen years is crowded a volume of facts that are the best interpretation of the thought of our Church in this legislation that has been criticised by some members of other communions. Mark some of these facts: The bishops transferred zealous and talented ministers from good charges in the North, who have thrown their whole strength into the work among the lowly; every benevolent and connectional society has uniformly and liberally aided that work; a score or more of commodious college buildings, and the grand work in them, now tell the story of a true charity and unselfish devotion of which in a coming day they will be monumental; the bishops superintend these Conferences, preside in their annual sessions, hold cabinet-meetings with their presiding elders, and station the preachers, just the same as in other Conferences; and more than all as an exponent of honest and cordial recognition, these Conferences have had their delegates in the last four General Conferences, holding an equal place, having an equal voice with other delegates in the only legislative and absolutely supreme body of our Church. Are not such facts as these, which add to the real glory of our history, in harmony with the legislation of our Church? Does not her controlling thought and spirit determine both her law and her administration? Do they not both emanate from the one all-dominating Gospel sentiment—good will to man?

Other denominations have done, and are doing, well for the freed people; we honor them for their work, and rejoice in their success; but standing in the presence of the work of our Church in our "new Southern field," as well as in the other Southern States, keeping in view the results I have mentioned—the results of her itinerant system, her doctrinal teachings, her conference relations, her connectional polity, her organized benevolences, her religious literature, her educational institutions, her Church life—in a word, with the results of her manifold yet unified work among the colored people and in their behalf in view, I feel warranted in expressing the belief that those who are nurtured and trained by our Church, built up into a free Christian manhood and womanhood by her means, will be foremost among the leaders of their people in all fields of intellectual and moral activity until they reach by culture and achievement the same unquestioned equality in the sphere of cultivated talents and social attainments that our Church has demanded for them and accorded to them in Christian privileges and personal rights.

While I have chosen to discuss, on this occasion, the mission of our Church in its relation to the colored people, I am not unmindful of the importance of her work among the white people. The opening to this field was providential; the work has features of special interest, and has been attended with many gratifying results. In the Conferences maintained through all changes in the border States, there has been a steady and solid growth. Beyond these lie the belt of eight Conferences in the central South, stretching from the Atlantic to the Indian Territory and to the south-west, including Texas. In all these white Conferences, as elsewhere, the connectional polity, doctrinal teaching, and Wesleyan spirit of our Church have determined the results of her work.

Nineteen years ago (1863), within the border Slave States, our Church had 332 effective preachers, 60,436 white and 16,238 colored members, and 6,988 white and 1,015 colored probationers. Now within the sixteen Southern States she has thirteen white Conferences, with 693 effective preachers and 179,847 members and probationers; fourteen colored Conferences, with 678 effective preachers and 181,007 members and probationers; and three mixed Conferences (the Florida in the extreme southeast, the St. Louis and the Missouri in the extreme north-west, of the field), with 218 effective preachers and 40,966 members and probationers—in all, thirty co-equal Conferences, with 1,589 effective preachers and 401,820 members and probationers.

Even far more important than this fivefold increase in ministry and membership is the fact that the doctrinal views, the Christian faith, the spiritual experiences, the moral habits, the Church life of these people, white and colored, are what they have become under the teaching, inspiration, and molding influence of our Church. Thus trained, they must be an active and conspicuous element in developing in the South those better civil, social, and religious conditions in which all men shall alike enjoy every inherent and conventional right.

THE NEW SOUTH—WHAT SHALL IT BE?

BY REV. J. C. HARTZELL, D. D.,
ASSISTANT CORRESPONDING SECRETARY.

Has the conflict of diverse civilizations in our nation ended? To those who think it has, the following words are specially spoken:

A LITTLE HISTORY.

Our fathers, wise as we, thought this conflict past when, by constitutional provision, the slave-trade was to stop in 1808. Later on, our statesmen said all was settled, when, in 1820, by what was called a compromise, that part of our national domain north of a certain line was dedicated to freedom, and that south of it to slavery. Still later, when popular sovereignty triumphed, the end was announced. President Buchanan, in his inaugural address, March 4, 1857, referring to this conflict and to the Dred Scott decision—of which he knew, but which was not made public till two days later—said, "Every thing of a practical nature had been settled," and announced that "agitation would cease." Soon afterward came the John Brown tragedy and the crashing thunders of Fort Sumter.

Not long after that declaration of Buchanan the voice of God was heard in the Far West, speaking through the immortal Lincoln: "A house divided against itself can not stand. . . . The American nation must be either all free or all slave." That was the beginning of which Appomattox was the end.

But did Appomattox end all? To overwhelm the military power of a nation is one thing; to change their civilization, quite another. The former is the work of a day, the latter requires generations. England long ago conquered Ireland with bayonet and cannon; but the Ireland of to-day is no more a part of England, in fact, than when it surrendered on the battle-field.

The civilization for which the South fought is the growth of many generations. The convictions underlying it are profound, and, being sanctified by the Church, are a part of her religion.

Appomattox brought military defeat: but what of the conflict of opinion and thought and conviction; and what of the tremendous uplift in education of brain and conscience necessary to remove the results of the old and bring in a new civilization, having in it, for all alike, whatever freedom rightly means?

CONFEDERACY OF SOUTHERN IDEAS.

The Confederacy of Southern States, with organized Congress and marshaled armies, is gone. In its stead is another Confederacy, more potent by far, and that is *the Confederacy of Southern ideas*. Armies can be overwhelmed. Ideas and convictions only die with a race. In America ideas rule. The supreme place of power is in the will of the individual voter. Governors and Presidents simply execute that will. Southern ideas gave the South—what her leaders called and rejoiced in—a "semi-feudal civilization," where the few were rich and ruled, the blacks were slaves, and the many whites were ignorant and obeyed. Those ideas, crystallized into that civilization, ruled the nation for generations. Failing to rule, it sought to ruin. Its methods were secession and war. They failed. What next? Read the words of her statesmen, as voiced by Alexander H. Stephens, upon his election to the United States Senate from Georgia in 1866:

"Secession was tried. That has failed. . . . Our only alternative now is either to give up all hope of constitutional liberty, or retrace our steps, and to look for its vindication and maintenance in the forums of reason and justice, instead of in the arena of arms; in courts and halls of legislation, instead of on the field of battle."

That was a few months after Appomattox. It was a keynote as clear and as significant as was ever spoken by a great leader. It outlined the policy of the Confederacy of Southern ideas as clearly as did secession and war that of the Confederacy of States.

DEVELOPMENT, POWER.

The victories of peace in the South since Appomattox have been many and splendid.

Christian benevolence from the North has triumphed. Twenty-five millions of dollars have gone into the South since the war, a free gift, out of the heart of the North, to rebuild her waste places among her poor. Consecrated men and women, the bearers of that gift, have sanctified it with their sympathies, prayers, tears, and blood. A distinguished Southern author and educator says: "Suppose these Northern teachers had not come, that nobody had taught these Negroes, set free, and citizens! The South would have been uninhabitable by this time." A prominent Southern judge, after sitting a day in our Louisiana Conference, said to me: "This is Christianity, this is civilization. What I have seen to-day gives me, for the first time since freedom, hope for the Negro."

The many, instead of the few, are becoming land-owners. In 1880 there were 310,795 more farm-owners in six Southern States than in 1870. In Mississippi the number of land-owners increased 50 per cent; in Virginia, 60 per cent; in North Carolina, 68; in Louisiana, 70; in Arkansas, 91; in Georgia, 98; in Alabama, 102; in Florida, 129; and in Texas, 185 per cent. This increase has been largely among the Negroes. Governor Jarvis, of North Carolina, says the average value of land is as much in the South now as before the war. Agricultural methods are improving. Free labor has raised 10,000,000 more bales of cotton in fifteen years than was raised in the same time during slavery's palmiest days. Thus does freedom make the very soil laugh with joy.

Mines and mineral wealth, factories and railroads, are being developed. Millions of wealth are pouring out of the mountain sides. At Birmingham, Alabama, alone, $5,000,000 are invested in iron-works. Already we hear talk of competing with New England in manufacturing. Hundreds of millions of capital have gone into Southern railroads.

The Negro has shared in the advance. His increase in numbers has been great—35 per cent by births alone, as against 29 per cent among the whites of the nation by births and immigration, from 1870 to 1880. He numbers 6,500,000 in the South, and has gained since emancipation $100,000,000 in taxable property. That is only $15 apiece. So they are yet poor, but the beginning is a good one. Many negroes are getting homes where father, mother, and children dwell in love, and into which the life-giving streams of intelligence and piety are pouring from the school-house and church. How freedom feeds and clothes her poorest children!

Another victory is the revival of sentiment in favor of popular education, not for the few only, but for all. The South is coming to believe in public schools. Negro education is being advocated and begun. Out of 3,899,961 white school population in the sixteen Southern States in 1880, 2,215,674 were enrolled in public schools; and out of 1,803,259 Negro school population, 784,709 were enrolled. The same year the South gave $12,475,644 for public schools. These are encouraging figures. The work done is but little more than a beginning; but such a beginning in so few years is remarkable, and promises much for the future.

The old Southern Churches are feeling the impulse of the new life. Freed from the nightmare of Negro chattelism, the Southern pulpit is speaking out more plainly upon questions of practical reform. It is freeing itself from the domination of political rule, which was absolute under slavery. Home and foreign missionary work, and local Church extension and educational movements, are being enlarged.

Every lover of God and our country rejoices in these and other evidences of a new and better civilization in the South. The South has arisen from the dust and ashes of mortifying defeat, and stands before the nation and the world, a wonderful illustration of the recuperative and self-adjusting power of the Anglo-Saxon.

THESE VICTORIES PECULIARLY SOUTHERN.

The South has had no immigration from foreign lands, while nearly a million a year have poured into the Northern States. Neither have many gone into the South from the North, except into Western Texas and Florida. The cry of "carpet-baggers" in the South was a political cry, which did its work well for them who used it. It is said that there are more carpet-baggers from the South in New York and Philadelphia than there are in the whole South from the whole North. This is providential. The time has not come for large immigration into the South. Many questions must first be settled among the diverse peoples of that section, as Appomattox left them. The South has already too much labor for its capital and brains. Railroads, factories, mines, hand implements, and common schools are improving its brain and capacity; and the teachings of God's providence are helping to solve the question of free labor.

"WITH MALICE TOWARD NONE, WITH CHARITY FOR ALL."

In studying the sentiments and spirit of the New South, it is scarcely necessary to remark that the sincerity or bravery of her people are not questioned. Her Churches are one with the North in all great essentials of doctrine. The faith of our common Bible inspired and saved the Christian boy in gray, as it did the Christian boy in blue. Still, the differences of civilization in the sections are substantial and far-reaching. These differences rest upon convictions which permeate every phase of thought, belief, and activity. These are the more difficult to comprehend because both sections are so nearly the same in many essentials of civilization, and the comminglings of trade and social life are so complex. And still, again, these differences relate to racial, social, and governmental questions of the gravest magnitude, and about which the best men in no clime or nation have the same belief. The old semi-feudal civilization before the war was not altogether bad; nor are the sentiments of the North at war with the South faultless.

Admit and remember all these points, still the fact remains that for generations the conflict of civilizations between the sections has gone on, and that many of the essential differences are as marked since Appomattox as before.

THE QUESTION STATED.

The new South will have commercial prosperity, agricultural development, great political power, a vast and increasing population, and in time her masses will be educated. To the politician, the leaders in trade and finance, or the multitudes dependent on them, these are enough. Not so with the Christian patriot, philanthropist, and statesman. The South was rich and prosperous when, with slavery supreme, she marshaled her armies to destroy the nation. The question is, Shall the parties and power and wealth and increasing intelligence of the New South be permeated and directed by the convictions and ideas of the old sectional and race-prejudiced South? Negro chattelism is gone, but American race prejudice, the basis and defense of slavery, remains. Shall the new South make its fetters only the more powerful and its effects the more far-reaching and permanent? This is a specimen question of many.

Mr. Calhoun said in the United States Senate, in 1840, " We regard slavery as the most safe and stable basis for free institutions in the world." On that the old South was a unit, and ruled and fought.

Senator Lamar, of Mississippi, speaking in the same place in 1881, with Negro chattelism gone, and sixteen years after Appomattox, said;

"There is no solid South as a factor in legislation; but there is one point in which the South is solid, and will remain so. It is solid for the defense and protection of its own civilization, its own society, its own religion."

On this the new South is a unit to-day, and goes forth to do battle and rule, " in the forums of reason and justice," and " in courts, and halls of legislation."

MARSHALING FORCES.

The forces of the Confederacy of Southern ideas are better in hand than were those of Lee and his generals. There are no factions. A single purpose, more powerful because largely ideal, animates and directs all.

The South has " its own civilization, its own society, its own religion." Mr. Lamar knew what he said. No one doubts it who knows any thing of Southern thought or society. One orator, in 1875, before the University of Virginia, said:

"The *Mayflower* freight, under the laws of England, was heresy and crime. The Jamestown emigrant was an English freeman, loyal to his country and his God, with England's honor in his breast, and with English piety in his soul. . . . These two people . . . nominally read the same Bible; but, like the offspring of the Syrian princess, they were two manner of people, and they could not coalesce or commune."

From this beginning he traced the development of Southern civilization till the war, and says that in that contest:

"Our stake was not only land and liberty, but all the forms, modes, purposes, habitudes, and sympathies of social organisms, and sealed to us by sacrifices of blood."

As says this orator, so say the Southern press, pulpit, poets, and colleges. The exceptional words are so rare as to awaken national comment when heard. The phrase, " our people," in the South, is the popular expression of this sentiment.

The South is determined that whatever of political, commercial, or educational prosperity it may have shall be utilized in perpetuating its own civilization, society, and religion.

In 1883, eighteen years after Appomattox, before an immense

audience, in Baltimore, at an army reunion, a prominent Southern orator said:

"I trust that every faithful soldier of Virginia is ready to exclaim with me—if I ever disown, repudiate, or apologize for the cause for which Lee fought and Jackson died, let the lightnings of heaven blast me, and the scorn of all good men and true women be my portion."

The speaker could not proceed for some time because of the deafening applause, led by a United States Senator and other prominent men on the platform. That scene is being repeated scores of times every year in the cities and towns of the whole South. One of three things must be true. These orators and the multitudes who cheer them are fools or hypocrites or honest men. Every thing indicates that they are honest men, and have judgment and character, and know what their words and acts signify. And what is more, back of their acts and words, inwrought into their lives, are convictions of a hundred years' growth.

The South is a unit politically. Whether in Congress or State Legislature, in party caucus or in private confab, north of the Ohio or south of it, the rule is well-nigh absolute—the Southerner stands for his people and their cause. He makes Southern ideas so much his own that when you do not accept them you reject him, and to oppose them is to insult him.

There is an organized movement to give the South its own literature. In the old semi-feudal civilization a man could be hung for aiding in the circulation of literature which would "have a tendency" to make the slaves or free Negroes discontented. The methods now are different. Southern historical societies are organized. These,

"Having enrolled among its members the true exponents of Southern honor and intelligence," will be "powerful to repel the insidious advance of those vicious principles which are now so fearfully undermining the civilization of the North." These societies are "to urge her surviving children to vindicate the great principles for which she [the South] fought."

"If they [children] are made to comprehend the origin, progress, and culmination of that great controversy between the antagonistic sections, which began in the Convention of 1787 and ended, for the time being, at Appomattox in 1865, they can not fail to see that truth, right, justice, were on the side of their fathers, and they will surely strive to bring back to the Republic those cardinal principles on which it was founded, and on which alone it can exist."

"Maid, mother, and wife gave freely to that country [Southern

Confederacy] the most cherished objects of their affections. It is theirs to teach our children that their fathers were neither traitors nor rebels."

These words are quoted from a United States Senator. Leading men in state and Church are officers or influential members of these societies. They have branch organizations in chief cities of the South, proposing "to publish, regularly and systematically, all contributions which elucidate the truth, reflect the glory, and maintain the principles involved in the late war."

On the same line are the histories of Stephens and Pollard and Davis, biographies of Southern generals and statesmen and divines, also monthly and quarterly magazines, histories of Southern States and Churches, and addresses and sermons on fast days— all breathing the same spirit and teaching the same doctrines. To this must be added the entire secular and religious press of the South, with only a few unimportant exceptions. Is it not a remarkable fact, that in the midst of one-third of the people of this nation, there is hardly a respectable daily or weekly secular paper not sectionally Southern in sentiment?

The rising generation in the South is being instructed in sectional ideas and prejudices. Senator Hampton calls upon "maid, mother, and wife to teach the children;" and school histories teaching, for example, that "Louisiana is one of the sovereign States of the United States," are put into the public and private schools. In some cases, by formal vote of county committees, teachers of public schools are compelled to certify that they are Democrats and will work with that party. I have certified copies of such pledges. In a prospectus of a Kentucky college it is said: "The Southern is the highest type of civilization this continent has seen;" and, "We offer a first-class female college for the South, and solicit Southern patronage." Thus is the conflict transferred to the forum of reason.

Social influences are made to conserve sectional ideas. The proverbial hospitality of the South is a reality, up to the divergence of sentiment respecting Southern civilization. Especially is this true of "maid, mother, wife." Local military organizations crystallize about some remnant of a Confederate army or regiment, and about these cluster powerful social influences. The tyranny of social law is not dreamed of in the North as it is seen in daily operation in the South. The monumental associations are another factor. They are everywhere, and command the fairest and bravest women and men in every community. Their purpose is manifest, and the educating power upon the youth—from the evening festival to the dedicatory oration in the presence of applauding thousands—can not fail to be great.

Southern pulpits and Churches largely lead in this movement. This adds the intensity of religious conviction. One fact, known to all, illustrates this point. Every Southern Church scouts the idea of organic union with its Northern branch. Why? Because to the Southern Churchly mind organic union with a Northern Church would in some way mean disloyalty to Southern civilization. The arguments of Southern statesmen and ministers, each in their spheres, are the same. The "constitutional liberty" of the one is called "constitutional Church polity" by the other. Each in his place stands with Mr. Lamar, the Southern Methodist statesman, "for the defense and protection" of their own "civilization, society, religion."

THE CHALLENGE GIVEN.

This marshaling of forces by the Confederacy of Southern ideas is just what any brave and intelligent people would do, after military defeat. The heroism of the movement must command the respect of all. What Mr. Stephens in 1866 stated as a suggestion, is now a unified and powerful movement. A few months since, before a vast audience in New Orleans, a distinguished divine, speaking for a Southern historical society, said:

"Can any one deny that great and fundamental principles lay at the heart of the civil war in which the two sections of this country were lately engaged? It is due to historic truth that both should be set forth by the advocates who were willing to submit them to the gauge of battle. I would have the Southern expounder and the Northern expounder stand face to face, as did Lee and Grant at Appomattox, and argue 'the case before the nations of the earth."

These are not the words of tyros in philosophy or eloquence or statesmanship, or of fanatics mad with theories, or of spiteful antagonists overwhelmed in battle. They are the words of men who represent stalwart and tremendous forces, imbedded in the hearts of millions, for whom they speak.

The challenge has gone forth. The purpose of Southern leaders is open, manly, and brave. It is to vindicate the old South, by making the new South as sectional and Southern and dominant as was its predecessor.

THE LINES OF BATTLE.

The Confederacy of Southern ideas does not contemplate secession or war. These have been tried. Neither does it propose to re-establish Negro chattelism, nor pay the Confederate debt or redeem the Confederate bonds. More fundamental and far-reaching questions are at the front.

The issues to-day, as before Appomattox, all center in two— *the relation of the State to the Nation, and the Negro.* All other questions upon which the South and the North do not substantially agree center in these.

The Superintendent of Public Education in Louisiana refused to adopt a certain text-book because, as he said, "it taught the heresy that this is a nation, instead of a confederation of States." That puts the issue practically. That supreme heresy in American politics, "State sovereignty," as distinguished from national authority, is the "constitutional liberty" for which the South fought "in the arena of arms," and failing there, renews the conflict "in the forums of reason and justice."

This is not a question of party politics. To say so is to trifle with a momentous issue, over which contending Christian armies have fought, and multitudes of noble men have died. This question involves all the duties and responsibilities of the holiest patriotism. It is this dogma that gives the South its sectionalism. Some State constitutions, in defining treason, magnify the State and minify or disregard the nation. National legislation is wanted which builds levees, custom-houses, and increases power; but when that legislation exalts the nation, as distinguished from the State, the South resents it, and will either defeat it or neutralize its power if possible. Northern ideas and capital are welcomed for all possible commercial purposes, and also Northern methods and money for educational work: but when either that capital, or those ideas or methods, or that benevolence are used to develop thought and conviction that shall be national, instead of Southern and sectional, they are not wanted.

The other great issue relates to the Negro—*not his re-enslavement, but that he shall be kept in what the South regards as his God-appointed subordinate relation to the white man.*

The Southerner will protect and defend a Negro as long as he "is in his place," just as a man will defend his favorite dog in his place. But if the dog should insist on eating with the family he will be punished. So, if the Negro will be satisfied with his subordinate relations to the white race all is well: but if he asks the recognition due to real manhood, even if he has more brains and culture than his white neighbor, he is then an "impudent nigger" forcing a "race issue," and must be "watched" and, if need be, "advised to leave."

The illustrations of this sentiment and of its enforcement are seen everywhere in the South. In politics the law announced is, "This is the white man's government;" and whatever is necessary to assure this must be advocated or excused. As to "civil rights," the Negro shall have such only as his "proper" relations to the whites allow. The intermarriage of the races is made a heinous crime. Socially, the Negro is to be forbidden recognition. As a leader in Southern society said to one of our cultured lady teachers in the South, "You treat kitchen people as equals, and we, of course, can not recognize you." In educational matters, separate schools for the races are insisted upon, and the quality and quantity of instruction must be such as will best fit the Negro for his "proper sphere." In Church matters, there must be separate organizations. So on through the whole list of relations touching the Negro.

Slavery was to have been the corner-stone of the Southern Confederacy of States; the permanent subordination of the Negro to the white race, irrespective of his progress or character, is now the corner-stone of the Confederacy of Southern ideas. As one Southern divine puts it, "The relations of the races are fixed, and will remain so, although it may bring agitation, and possibly bloodshed."

BULL RUN OVER AGAIN, AND WORSE.

The late war opened with a Bull Run defeat to the national army; and we are told that, had the Confederates known how great their victory really was, they could have made Washington their capital instead of Richmond. The new Confederacy has made Washington its capital, and already commands many and powerful influences in national "courts and halls of legislation."

At the outbreak of the rebellion, so fully had the nation been educated and committed to extreme State-rights doctrines that many loyal statesmen doubted the constitutional right of coercion.

Only the higher law of self-preservation fully aroused the enthusiasm of the nation. To-day the South, solid as a section, lacking only a fraction of a majority in Congress, and having one hundred and fifty-three of the two hundred and one electoral votes necessary to elect a President, unchanged in sentiment on the two great issues between the sections, is again a part of the nation, each State having full right to every advantage guaranteed by those very State-rights doctrines which the same section forced upon the nation in its defense of slavery.

Current events show how well this vantage ground is being used. Study the debates in Congress, or the conflicts between the government and the Southern States in the collection of internal revenue, or the "investigations" of political murders in the South, or the attempts to punish violators of national laws in election matters. It has come to pass that the nation is absolutely powerless to protect voters in the South, no matter how open may be the frauds or how vicious the persecutions.

Then, again, the nation supposed that, in addition to giving the Negro his freedom and his citizenship, it had by constitutional amendment provided a way, when necessary, of interfering directly for his protection in his civil rights. Hence the civil-rights legislation. These laws have had but little, if any, practical force in the South, but they stood as a pledge of national faith. These are now, eighteen years after Appomattox, declared unconstitutional. Senator Brown, of Georgia, as head of the new Georgia railroad syndicate, announces that, "under the altered condition of things made by the civil-rights decision, Negroes must ride in Negro cars." So as to all the points involved. Instead of seeking to know how the South can insure the civil rights of the Negro, every step is toward fixing permanently, by law and custom, his subordinate relations, and the nation is powerless to say a word.

A white Virginian takes a bride, in whose veins African blood gives a somber tinge, perhaps, to the blood of some "oldest and best citizen." They are married in Washington, under the shadow of the Capitol, according to the laws of Christian America. They recross the Potomac to their home. Virginia law arrests them, and they are sent to the penitentiary, and the Supreme Court of that same Christian America can only say, Virginia's laws must be obeyed. Laws similar to those of Virginia are in nearly all

Southern States. Where no such laws are in force, then mob law does the work. In Mississippi such a bridal party was followed and shot to death. The community approved the deed as fully as did the Israelites the work of Phinehas, when he thrust his javelin through Zumri and his Midianitish bride, Cozbi. Justice Harlan, in his dissent from the civil-rights decision, said:

"In view of what the people of this country wished to accomplish, what they sought to accomplish, and what they believed they had accomplished by means of this legislation, he must express his dissent from the opinion of the court."

Bishop Wiley says:

"This decision puts the nation back twenty years. I had begun to spell nation with capital N, but now I will stop it."

This decision is only a specimen step in the march to power of the Confederacy of Southern ideas, in the forum. As Everett said of all the States fifty years ago, can now be said with special force of the Southern States:

"We have called them into a full partnership in the government, and the course of events has put crowns upon their heads and scepters in their hands, and we must abide the result."

Only to-day (November, 1883) a Richmond paper warns the South not to be in too much of a hurry in dictating policies and measures for the nation through the next Democratic National Convention. It says:

"The time has not come for us to act. When we have the wealth, the population, and the power to enforce our rights, then will be the time to put forth our strength and take with a strong hand what now we could only ask as a favor, and which, even if granted, might prove utterly valueless."

THE SOUTH MUST BE RIGHTLY EDUCATED.

Let no one misunderstand me. What I have said I here repeat, and add to it. The South is doing just what any intelligent and brave people would do who had been overwhelmed on the battle field; and I believe its present attitude toward the nation and the Negro displays more commendable diplomacy and heroism than were shown in secession and war. I would take no constitutional right from any State. Neither do I now question the correctness of the late decisions in the local and supreme national courts.

Nor do I regret that every Southern State stands the equal with every other State in the Republic. Neither do I forget that on nearly every point I have named exceptional voices are heard. Nor have I failed to study the difficulties of the Negro problem in every part of the South. Nor do I fail to make account of the influences of commercial and social intermingling of the sections, and the growth of commerce and secular education in the South.

On the other hand, I remember that exceptional voices and factors were heard and felt before 1860, and that when the crisis came these only added breadth and power to the movement to destroy the nation. *Now, as then, trade has no conscience or country, and education may teach treason or loyalty, sectionalism or nationality.* During the war, when a native Union man in Louisiana was being taken beyond the lines by a Confederate vigilance committee, he asked, "Gentlemen, what law of my country have I broken, that I should be banished from my State?" The reply was, "We are Louisianians first, and Americans second." That is the key to Southern statesmanship in State and Church—Southern first, American second. To the South, disloyalty to the State is treason. And this is not fanaticism or infatuation, but principle, and must be met as such, and supplanted or obeyed. Compromise there can not be.

An old gentleman, after listening to an address on our Southern educational work, said to me: "My oldest son lies buried at Vicksburg; and having given him, I can not see your work fail. Put me down for a hundred, and my wife for ten dollars." That man's wisdom and patriotism is a model for the nation. The new South, with its rising power, must be educated out of its sectionalism. Its literature, its politics, its pulpits, its universities, its public schools, and its social life must be permeated with a national instead of a sectional patriotism. This is the work of generations, but it must be done. Some good beginnings have been made.

Respecting the Negro question, the issue and duty are equally plain and imperative. With the South, slavery was a matter of principle, intensified by religious conviction. So, to-day, the permanent subordination of the Negro is a matter of principle, intensified by religious conviction. Whatever was necessary to protect slavery was done and justified; and whatever will be necessary to "keep the Negro in his place" will be attempted, even to bloodshed.

Speaking of the violent measures used to subordinate the Negro vote in Mississippi, a Southern Methodist minister remarked, in the hearing of a friend of mine, "Sorry that such harsh measures had to be used, but it was necessary." These is a specimen conservative view.

In slavery, Christians and philanthropists in the South did what they could for the Negro's improvement, consistent with that relation. So now, in his new relation, some, and perhaps more, will labor for his good among Southern white people, provided "the absolute dominance of the Anglo-Saxon"—as a Southern writer has just put it—is maintained. When Gail Borden, of national fame and utility, was on his death-bed, he said to a friend who was a teacher among the Negroes, "Do n't forsake the freedmen, and God won't forsake you." God has taught this nation that it must not forsake the Negro.

The South must be rightly educated. The challenge of the new Confederacy, as voiced by that New Orleans divine, must be accepted. The "Northern expounder and the Southern expounder" must "stand face to face, as did Lee and Grant at Appomattox." *That is, they must meet each other on Southern soil.* In the Church and school, on the rostrum and in legislative halls, in books and papers and tracts, and at the ballot-box—in every proper way and place—let diverse convictions, sentiments, and thoughts meet on these great questions. The sectional, race-prejudiced South must be supplanted by a national and free South, where dominance of individual or race shall be only by virtue and intelligence.

In this great work many influences already active in the South will be powerful. Chief among these is the Christian South, seeking to know the teachings of God's providence and to follow them. If the Christian North and South could meet, free from mutual distrust, and together in the name of the Master combine faith and prayer and work for the uplifting of the ignorant and needy masses of that section, how glorious would be the results! In such a crucible of sacrifice and toil the errors of conviction or prejudice, no matter by whom held, would go, and only the truth remain. It is to just such a united work that the whole nation is called by the highest patriotism and the divinest philanthropy. For the South to say, "This is our field," in the presence of a work which it is not doing, and can not do for generations, if at all, is worse than absurd. The claim of the South concerning the Negro, that "we are his guardians," is equally absurd. The American nation and Church are the guardians of every citizen under the flag. No section can claim any guardianship over the Negro, except as by grand faith and tremendous effort it excels in educating and saving him. Just so as to the illiterate and needy masses among the whites of the South. The whole nation must help save them, because the South is not doing it, and can not, and because they need and must have the ideas and convictions of a newer and better civilization. Thus it is that *the appalling illiteracy of the South may be a providential factor* for the unification and redemption of all. Any "fraternity," in Church or state, which would keep the heart and benevolence and missionary zeal and methods of the North out of the South, is in league with treason to the best interests of Christ's kingdom, if not of the nation also.

THE NEW SOUTH—WHAT SHALL IT BE?

Shall it be the old South over again in sectionalism and race prejudice, only more powerful in ruling the nation and in riveting an un-American and un-Christian social, civil, and political bondage upon millions of our brothers and sisters, more galling than slavery itself? Whatever of patriotism or philanthropy were in putting down rebellion and destroying slavery are in these questions also. They were moral issues; so are these. Patriotism without God in it is worthless, and philanthropy without Christ in it is selfishness.

More than any other organized moral power in America, the Methodist Episcopal Church is responsible for the proper answer to this question. Vast in wealth and numbers and peerless in organization and missionary zeal, this Church, more than any other, is national in her organization and methods. Already two millions—about equally divided between the races—are in her communion and congregations, on what was slave territory. Her schools and colleges, with more than six thousand five hundred young men and women in them—every one of them loyal to Christ and his children, and their country as well—are in every Southern State. The imperative demand now is to enlarge these schools, so that speedily there may be intelligent and Christian ministers, teachers, physicians, mechanics, and social leaders among the Negroes and ignorant whites of the South. Could the Church have a million dollars at once for this work, how speedy and glorious would be the results!

www.ingramcontent.com/pod-product-compliance
Lightning Source LLC
Chambersburg PA
CBHW022133160426
43197CB00009B/1262